E-Strategy

Michael J. Cunningham

T0313454

- Fast track route to developing effective and profitable e-strategies for organizations.

- Covers all the key techniques for development of a coherent and effective e-strategy for an organization.

- Examples and lessons from some of the world's most successful businesses, including eBay, General Electric and Richard Branson's Virgin, plus ideas from the smartest thinkers, including Michael Porter, Thomas Hagal and Patricia Seybold.

- Includes a glossary of key concepts and a comprehensive resources guide

essential management thinking at your fingertips

Copyright © Capstone Publishing 2002

The right of Michael J. Cunningham to be identified as the author of this work has been asserted in accordance with the Copyright, Designs and Patents Act 1988

First published 2002 by
Capstone Publishing (a Wiley company)
8 Newtec Place
Magdalen Road
Oxford OX4 1RE
United Kingdom
http://www.capstoneideas.com

CIP catalogue records for this book are available from the British Library and the US Library of Congress

ISBN 1-84112-214-9

Printed and bound in Great Britain by CPI Antony Rowe, Eastbourne

This book is printed on acid-free paper

Substantial discounts on bulk quantities of Capstone books are available to corporations, professional associations and other organizations. Please contact Capstone for more details on +44 (0)1865 798 623 or (fax) +44 (0)1865 240 941 or (e-mail) info@wiley-capstone.co.uk

Contents

Introduction to ExpressExec

ExpressExec is 3 million words of the latest management thinking compiled into 10 modules. Each module contains 10 individual titles forming a comprehensive resource of current business practice written by leading practitioners in their field. From brand management to balanced scorecard, ExpressExec enables you to grasp the key concepts behind each subject and implement the theory immediately. Each of the 100 titles is available in print and electronic formats.

Through the ExpressExec.com Website you will discover that you can access the complete resource in a number of ways:

» printed books or e-books;
» e-content – PDF or XML (for licensed syndication) adding value to an intranet or Internet site;
» a corporate e-learning/knowledge management solution providing a cost-effective platform for developing skills and sharing knowledge within an organization;
» bespoke delivery – tailored solutions to solve your need.

Why not visit www.expressexec.com and register for free key management briefings, a monthly newsletter and interactive skills checklists. Share your ideas about ExpressExec and your thoughts about business today.

Please contact elound@wiley-capstone.co.uk for more information.

Introduction to E-Strategy

What is the role of e-strategy in the modern world of business? This chapter considers the changing nature of e-strategy, including:

» why companies need to use e-strategy as a competitive weapon; and
» how e-strategy has become a metaphor for both success and failure in many organizations, but how it is needed to ensure success for almost any operation in the future.

This chapter examines:

» macro strategies;
» global strategies;
» communication strategies; and
» business improvement strategies.

How does e-strategy differ from mainstream strategy and why should I care? The answer is: a great deal. As we enter this next stage in the development of the marketplace, winners and losers have abounded. The market has now divided into three categories the types of organizations that use e-strategy and e-business tools and systems to support their efforts:

» only online;
» mainly offline; and
» hybrids (bricks-and-mortar).

The "only online" firms have been few and far between in terms of sheer visibility in the marketplace – the big ones include Amazon.com, Ameritrade, Monster.com, and Priceline.com.

E-strategy is the means to develop and change the way that a business or organization is operating by using e-business tools and techniques as the lever. In recent years, as the Internet and supporting technologies have surrounded us, many operations have been in maelstrom over the past several years, trying to figure out strategy, technology, and new business methods while the marketplace has been exploding and imploding. Today a more pragmatic view prevails. Organizations want to understand what works and what doesn't. They take best practices and learn from them rather than pioneering on their own. While some of the pioneers have benefited from their experimentation, others have lost out.

The development of strategies for organizations has been the topic of books and manuscripts for centuries. However, e-strategies are different because of the speed and quality of their impact.

Most operations are concerned with major components in the development of their strategies today. The challenges are manifold, but can be categorized into the following segments.

1 Macro strategies, that affect the big picture, are affected by geopolitical and economic factors and are longer term in nature.
2 Global strategies that affect the international nature and competitiveness of a product line or service.
3 Communications strategies.
4 Business improvement strategies:

4.1 sales;

4.2 marketing;

4.3 margin;

4.4 support;

4.5 penetration; and

4.6 speed of entrance to, and exit from, markets.

MACRO STRATEGIES

In the current state of development of these strategic areas, you could argue that most firms are paying little attention to the first one. Why? Most of us are too small to care about it, and while we certainly are concerned if consumer confidence or the stock market dips, it is more related to how other firms and buyers will affect our market. With the exception of the *Fortune 500*, most cannot influence these issues enough to spend a lot of time on them. There are global oil firms trying to keep fuel-efficient engines out of the marketplace so that demand for oil remains high in the West; Microsoft trying to avoid piracy of its software in developing countries; and huge multinationals looking for government bail-outs to keep themselves "competitive" in the marketplace.

Most of the real business world does not have any influence in these spheres. While industry associations and consortia will build organizations to "lobby" these areas, in the main most operations have to make their own strategies work, without much assistance from others. The exceptions are consortia that can create communities of buyers and sellers to "get ready" to optimize and change the way that their businesses are operating. Major changes such as these do not come easily, and need considerable momentum or business drivers to make them happen.

GLOBAL STRATEGIES

Selecting which markets we want to sell and distribute products into, however, is a very different ball game. In a world that has economies not just dependent on each other, but interdependent, global strategies have become very important. E-strategy can play a decisive role in how effective a global strategy is in roll-out, acceptance, and profitability. Many companies are making decisions to create a global presence much more rapidly as a result of the Internet and related technologies. E-business tools allow us to implement these changes in several areas simultaneously. Because global e-business strategies require an integrated approach to change, many elements have to be considered carefully before a complete and sophisticated roll-out can occur: the distribution model; product suitability; legal and pricing issues; localization and language factors; how the transaction will occur; and, finally, fulfillment and support of the product or service. Complex questions and issues, but ones where e-strategy can play a key role in making decisions and rolling out the solution.

COMMUNICATION STRATEGIES

Communication strategies can be viewed as a means to an end. In general, most e-business strategies are focused on either improving the way a business operates, in a measurable way, or changing the way a business communicates with its employees, customers, and business partners. Because the range of technologies and processes deployed in e-business solutions are so broad, we often become confused about the difference between these areas.

Communication strategies include:

» conferencing;
» delivery;
» applications;
» distribution;
» information push;
» information pull;
» research; and
» destination and collaboration sites.

You could argue that every company has a communication strategy; even though some may be very poor. Understanding that building a communications strategy can be a separate and perhaps easier way to create e-business benefits is often lost on managers who do not understand its potential. Communication improvements often have step improvements as they are adopted inside the organization. The construction industry, for example, has been slow to adopt the use of high-tech tools to assist communication between contractors, brokers, owners, and designers, despite the fact that many benefits can result. However, those that do use these tools have a considerable advantage over their peers, thereby giving them a considerable e-strategy lead in their industry segment. In many industries, electronic communication has become the norm, and e-mail, conferencing, and Web destinations assist considerably in the improvement of the business operation.

BUSINESS IMPROVEMENT STRATEGIES

The majority of e-strategy and e-business solutions have focused on individual business improvement programs and strategies. These are generally directed at a particular business function that is in need of improvement inside the operation. The pressure for these changes often comes from competitive elements. However, many organizations make these decisions based on improving work processes and internal systems, often to cut costs and perk up efficiency.

Whether driven by market conditions, or internal drive, there are a plethora of systems out there in the marketplace to improve business operations. Areas that are often targets for these systems include sales process and management, marketing and e-marketing initiatives, supply chain to improve margin and efficiencies, and customer and partner support systems to provide self-service answers to questions.

These systems are often used as a means to improve market positioning or allow a company to gain access to new markets. Sometimes the business improvement goes further, and changes the operation of a market, or the way consumers buy products.

This book is a good example of such a change. Traditional publishing models have followed a pattern unchanged in centuries. The book outline is prepared, a contract is signed with the author, development of copy, editing, production, printing, marketing, and distribution. Typical time-lines are around 9–12 months from beginning to end. Far too slow for time sensitive information contained in the *ExpressExec* series such as e-business. So taking advantage of electronic creation, production, and distribution technology, a new product, new process, and new business model emerges; one not bound by booksellers, marketing time-lines, and the events processes normally associated with marketing books. This example, like most examples in the e-business category, does not mean that the traditional book market is going away, but in the same way that Amazon has changed the way that many shop for books, the other e-business technologies will create new options for the presentation and delivery of information.

Regardless of whether your business is only online, mainly offline, or a hybrid, there are ways that your strategy can be improved by e-business technologies, process and destination sites. Determining the level of improvement can only come from looking at all aspects of the operation, not just the traditional things that have always worked, but by looking to innovate and change. Herein lies the gem of all strategies and tools to manage and operate a business: the desire – and the ability – to implement change.

What is E-Strategy?

E-strategy is an often misunderstood term. This chapter examines some of the definitions of e-strategy. It includes:

» what e-strategy is and how to take advantage of it;
» Gary Hamel and his view of e-strategy;
» value networks;
» Robert S. Kaplan and David P. Norton;
» translating strategy into operations; and
» frameworks.

To some, e-strategy is a layer, to others a tool, and some consider it a way of thinking. However, it should never be separated from mainstream strategy. E-strategy is a means to an end, and that end will be the successful implementation of the overall organizational or corporate strategy. In the early days of e-business (we are still there, of course), a separation of the existing organization to "new e-business" was considered the way to go. For some organizations this worked, for many it failed. The reasons that many took this approach had nothing to do with whether e-strategy was right or wrong for the business, it was all based on whether the organization had the ability and willingness to change, along with a clear understanding of how to use the e-business technology that would support it. The "war stories" proving how this worked in some cases and failed in others now abound, and the strategic failure of many of these operations can be attributed to several key reasons:

» the business plan was flawed in the first place;
» the market was not ready for the product offering;
» there was not enough sustainable value proposition in the company's strategy;
» funding was inadequate to change the business model or reach some acceptable level of profitability; and/or
» the technology did not work.

We need to learn from the failures as well as the successes. Whether you consider e-strategy a layer, a business function, or a group of people in the organization, the most important issue to understand is that e-strategy should be tightly integrated with your overall strategic decisions and programs. Integration is key.

E-strategy is the use of electronic tools, networks, and systems (including the Internet), combined with process change, that will assist an organization in the support of its overall strategy.

GARY HAMEL

Gary Hamel is a founder and chairman of Strategos, a visiting professor at London Business School, and a research fellow at Harvard Business

School. Hamel has articulated his views regarding e-strategy and its development in his book *Leading the Revolution*.

His strategies and their development are based on conclusions from studying "gray-haired revolutionaries" who have been leading new online businesses and hybrid bricks-and-mortar businesses. Hamel challenges organizations to move into a mode of "continuous reinvention" of their business plans and operations; otherwise they risk either missing market opportunities or becoming victims of their competitors.

His view of e-strategy and business conditions today is based on:

» the age of incremental change is over. Therefore, being an incumbent in the marketplace does not hold the protections it once did;
» more innovation is required, because of diminishing returns on the traditional ways of improving business operations: re-engineering, cost-cutting, cutbacks that are based on keeping the business model the same, not changing the way the business is conducted;
» revolution is based on innovation in business concepts: radical "reconceptions" of existing business models in ways that create new value for customers, surprises for competitors, and new wealth for investors; and
» companies can reshape themselves into perpetually innovative organizations by continually engaging in a cycle of idea generation, experiments, assessments, and implementations.

In *Leading the Revolution*, Hamel provides examples of where this new thinking has worked and created disruption inside an industry, and brought value to the organization. Financial institutions such as Charles Schwab and Fidelity have changed the way that individuals deal with their savings. As a result, US banks have lost almost half their market share to these new online business models.

In the development of strategy, Hamel identifies the following four areas that need to interact effectively before "revolutionary" change can occur in an organization. He then goes on to suggest 10 rules for successful implementation of e-strategy, which are summarized below.

Customer interface

As the Internet has caused such a radical shift in the way that businesses interact with both producers and consumers, the means by which this dynamic interface is managed must, suggests Hamel, change to allow fulfillment, service, and support to be managed electronically. All successful e-strategies, in fact, have made extensive use of self-service tools and technologies.

Core strategy

Understanding an organization's core strategy is the fulcrum of any change management program. Hamel encourages us to question how we are doing business. Is our mission still relevant to our customer base today? Can we change our offerings to customers by extending the product lines? Such issues assist considerably in the development of a core strategy that will drive all the connections around the operation.

Strategic resources

The strategic resources of an organization comprise three major components:

» core competencies;
» strategic assets; and
» core processes.

These are the fabric of change and how it will be brought to the organization. Obviously, any change in strategy should try to leverage these skills and tools, but sometimes a lack of resources in one area can lead to acquiring those skills in other ways, through acquisition of other businesses or hiring appropriate staff, or acquiring resources to get the new job done.

The core competencies of an organization are what the organization knows and can develop and deliver. They may be skills and knowledge about a particular industry, or a more general skill, such as the ability to develop software products. The strategic assets are what the organization owns, including intellectual capital. Many organizations are now beginning to understand the importance of managing the intellectual capital and resources of the operation. Finally, there are the core processes, or how the company does business.

Value network

The value network, as Hamel describes it, is the coalitions that surround the operation and how it leverages them. Often organizations continue to look for new relationships to improve the way they are operating. Whether these relationships are with distributors, suppliers, business partners, etc., there is often much that can be achieved by optimizing and networking them. Some of the greatest success stories are based on exploiting the value network – for instance, Michael Dell has built a hugely successful computer firm based on this key principle.

Ten design rules for innovation

For e-strategy identification and implementation, Hamel recommends following these 10 rules.

1 **Unreasonable expectations** – set high goals and create an environment that will allow your staff to beat the industry growth average. Aim high and results will meet expectations.

2 **Elastic business definition** – look for ways to keep the definition of your business broad and flexible. Hamel cites Virgin as an example of a company that successfully spans industries by looking for ways in which it can innovate in other sectors even if it has no track record in that sector.

3 **A cause, not a business** – keeping the energy level of a business operation linked to a cause, not just the business issues, will keep staff motivated and customers interested.

4 **New voices** – it is important to listen to those in the organization who can make change happen, and quickly. Providing a means for these voices to be heard is key to success.

5 **An open market for ideas** – create an environment inside the organization where new ideas can not only be listened to, but can be heard.

6 **An open market for capital** – do not set up hurdles for new projects, particularly if the ideas and plans behind those projects are innovative, sustainable, and will generate financial benefits.

7 **An open market for talent** – good talent is drawn by innovation: staff will come to work for (and stay with) organizations with a solid compensation base and interesting and challenging work.

8 **Low-risk experimentation** – experiment, but do not necessarily take large risks. Hamel suggests being bold, but also encourages understanding how to manage the downsides if a risk does not pan out.

9 **Cellular division** – dividing into manageable cells provides organizations with the option of being large, but not necessarily slow.
Organizations such as Virgin have practiced this division throughout
their operations for many years.

10 **Personal wealth accumulation** – share the winnings with the
staff that have created them.

Hamel believes in linking these elements together in the development
of any successful e-strategy for an organization. Whether a dedicated
online operation or a hybrid, these principles have helped organizations
develop their solutions and effectively deliver them to market.

ROBERT S. KAPLAN AND DAVID P. NORTON

Kaplan and Norton have become famous for a strategy and manage-
ment development tool known as the "balanced scorecard". In late
2000, they released a book called *The Strategy-Focused Organization*
(Harvard Business School Press). Robert Kaplan is the Marvin Bower
Professor of Leadership Development at Harvard Business School, and
David Norton is president of Balanced Scorecard Collaborative, Inc.

Their work is included in this segment of the book because their
approach is to merge regular strategy and e-strategy into a common
measurable format. They aim to ensure that the strategy that is defined
is measurable, and that the metrics can then be used to modify and
refine the strategy. This takes strategy from a high level to operational
results, essential to success by any measure. Their premise is based on
this five-point plan, each of which will be looked at below.

1 Translate the strategy into operational terms.
2 Align the organization to the strategy.
3 Make strategy everyone's everyday job.
4 Make strategy a continual process.
5 Mobilize change through executive leadership.

Translate the strategy into operational terms

The first principle of Kaplan and Norton is to place the strategy at
the center of the organization's activities. Their focus is that strategy
has to be understood in order to implement it effectively. This guiding

principle follows their balanced scorecard approach, providing a means to describe and measure the results from tangible and intangible assets.

Four elements are measured and reviewed in the development of solutions with this approach. These are financial, customer, internal business processes, and learning and growth. The financial element takes the view of the investor and what a change in strategy means in empirical terms of fiscal growth, profitability, and risk. The customer view defines what this will mean to existing and new customers to create value from their perspective. Internal business processes are measured based on their ability to create shareholder and customer satisfaction. Learning and growth will review what has to be changed in order to ensure that the organization has what it takes to make these changes occur.

Each of these then has to be measured as a strategic focus is taken to make changes to the business, before being taken to the next stage where goals and metrics are added to ensure that results are going to occur.

Align the organization to the strategy

Ensuring that an organization's business functions are aligned and agreed in the goals, metrics, and desired results is very important to the balanced scorecard approach. In smaller organizations, where the dependencies are on short links and communication is often easier, alignment can occur more easily. In larger organizations, greater effort has to be taken to make this "linkage" stick. In the balanced scorecard approach, Kaplan and Norton suggest the use of "shared service units". These units may provide shared services such as manufacturing, real estate, distribution, or other services that are important to the overall business strategy. They also follow the pattern of using the balanced scorecard to set, measure, and monitor performance goals and ensure they are providing what was jointly agreed at the beginning of the process.

Make strategy everyone's everyday job

By developing and encouraging strategic awareness in the workplace, organizations can drive strategy and its change right into the workplace. This can only be done by getting buy-in and education of what the strategy is, why it is doing something, and how it will be measured. Kaplan and Norton suggest that the balanced scorecard is both the measurement and the instrument of change, but of course the advice to keep staff aware and aligned is good, regardless of the methodology used to change behavior. By building team objectives and goals from the program, as always, the devil is in the detail.

Make strategy a continual process

Several factors can assist in making strategy part of a continual process. The first stage is to link strategy with the budget, which ensures that the business goals are tied to the operational plan to make them work. Kaplan and Norton also recommend feedback systems and measurement to ensure that the work really gets done. Of course, there is no use developing any strategy and then "throwing our brains away." We have to continually modify, improve, revise, and remodel according to changing internal and external conditions.

Mobilize change through executive leadership

Trying to make major change flow through any organization without the support of the executives is like pushing water uphill. It will not work. Kaplan and Norton strongly recommend that operations ensure that their leaders lead ... and lead well. Some of the strategy actions for executives include:

» value propositions that lead customers to do more business with the company, and at high margins;
» target customers where profitable growth will occur;
» create and lead with innovations in products, services, and processes; and
» make the necessary investment in people and systems to enhance processes and delivery differentiated value propositions for growth.

FRAMEWORKS

The development of frameworks, as can be seen from the earlier examples in this chapter, can have many angles and approaches.

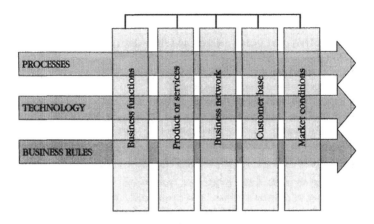

Fig. 2.1 Elements in e-strategy framework.

However, key to all successful strategies using e-business tools and systems is an integrated approach, as shown in Fig. 2.1.

An integrated approach will take all of these elements in a common framework and then determine the most effective method to create the results. The factors to be considered in an e-strategy versus a traditional (if there is such a thing) approach to strategy development are not huge. A surprising fact, perhaps, particularly when many in the market may tell you otherwise. The reality is that the only differences between e-strategy and the others are the dramatic way that a Go To Market strategy can be achieved, and the way that technology can either assist or create resistance within the organization that is planning to use it.

An effective approach to matching product with markets and channels uses a combination of strategic and tactical approaches. A five-step process captures data and provides an analysis mechanism to move to the next stage. Each one of these provides a measurement and means of scoring to determine the best solutions and alternatives. For e-business based strategies, this is particularly important, as the variables of business options and market conditions can change rapidly.

The major steps in this process include the following.

1 An analysis of available markets and their size (growth rates, expansion, etc.).
2 Understanding how e-business solutions or frameworks are likely to be accepted and used by this sector.
3 Rate of adoption likely from this sector.
4 Filter of the competition – where it is today and a prediction of how it might change over the next one to two years.
5 Mapping to the core capabilities of the operation to determine how best to build a solution to meet these needs.

By going through these processes, operations will start to see the beginning of programs, tools, and consultants from whom they can learn in the development of these solutions. Because many operations have failed, as well as others succeeding, there is much to be learned from these lessons. Certainly there is a need to start out with a strategy, supported by a good set of metrics and best practices, to ensure that your e-business program does not become a casualty.

The Evolution of E-Strategy

E-strategy has grown from an idea to a critical strategy for many organizations in less than five years. Few areas have had such a massive impact on business in such a short period as e-strategy and how to leverage it. This chapter examines the evolution of e-strategy, its use and successful implementation today. It includes:

» the history of a changed world;
» the infrastructure stage;
» exploitation stage;
» pragmatism; and
» "cluetrain" and other radical strategies.

HISTORY OF A CHANGED WORLD

The topic of e-strategy spawned experts at a more alarming rate than most. Because the only rule in e-business (for a while at least) was that there were no rules, some amazing prophecies and prophets hit the marketplace. By tying strategy to the e-commerce buzzword, it seemed to some to validate their approach, often without research, results, and experience. All has changed, however, now that organizations understand that earlier strategy work may not have been as flawed as was originally thought.

The reality of e-strategy and its very short history is that we are still learning. We have learned considerable lessons that should make e-strategy part of almost any organization's thinking, but we also need to put it into a context that is most relevant for each business. There is no one-size-fits-all in this world.

STAGE 1 – THE INFRASTRUCTURE STAGE

E-strategy roots are identified today from adoption phases of the Internet, 1995 onwards. However, e-strategy was used as a means to improve business-to-business (B2B) operations earlier than this, particularly with the use of EDI (Electronic Document Interchange) technologies from the 1970s onwards. The banking systems initially made use of this, but other network providers were developed to deliver information to those that needed it most via other private networks. These private networks were generally expensive at the time, so only high-value projects and applications were run across them. News networks, information services (such as Nexis/Lexus) and EDI systems were deployed across Value Added Networks (VANs) spread out across the globe. Most of these VANs remained intact as the primary way of "doing e-business" for several years. They extended their reach considerably as client/server computing technology came to market, linking the mainframe, mid-frame, and desktop PC technology in a short period.

As the Internet landed, a new means of doing business was emerging – even though the Internet had been around for many years (more than 20 at this stage), it was missing some consumable applications. As these arrived in the form of e-mail and the Web-browser, the

World Wide Web suddenly became accessible and affordable for many. It was only a matter of time before this was going to be *the* platform for the technology development of our future. During this time-frame, the Netscape and Microsoft wars started in earnest, and new Web-based development firms abounded in many different sectors, ranging from software, hosting, destination sites, and, of course, the mainstream portals.

STAGE 2 – THE EXPLOITATION STAGE

As the first stage reached its peak, the business moved into what we can now safely call the "exploitation stage". Exactly who exploited whom during this phase may still not be clear, but unquestionably everyone felt that there was a huge opportunity that could be exploited. The "land grab" then started, resulting in the largest injection of venture and other capital, as everyone raced to become a dot.com millionaire.

Of course, there were great development and success stories during these stages. IT hardware firms such as Cisco and EMC made billions in market capitalization as their stocks, margins, and revenues flew through the roof. Valuations became absurd in nature, but no one wanted to put a ceiling on an obviously artificial marketplace. Eventually the house came down in late 2000 and continued well into 2001. Firms that had gone from start-up darlings became "dogs" overnight; valuations moving from billions to pennies in a short period of time, with numbers somewhere in the region of $1.5trn in terms of capital lost, either on the markets, or through venture investments that failed or were devalued.

STAGE 3 – PRAGMATISM

We are now reaching another phase in the development of the Internet and the World Wide Web that may be scarier than the first round. While many organizations have already moved into the sector, using technology as a weapon in their arsenal, the rules continue to change and impact our actions for the future. More so than ever, the way in which we embrace e-business technologies will impact our potential for success, or increase our opportunity to stumble.

As managers and professionals in organizations today, we are faced with change as a normal way of life. We are in a world that expects us not only to know what is going to happen next, but to have predicted the solution so we are ready to exploit change when it comes. E-business tools can be a great catalyst to assist in the facilitation of this ''e-commerce'' change, but we have to understand the fundamentals in order to take the appropriate action. The technology confusion is still with us. We still have as many definitions of the subject as there are vendors and suppliers in the marketplace.

The very high failure rates of most IT projects continue to scare the best of us. According to more recent surveys, these are getting worse not better. I believe that one reason that this rate is so high is the poor integration of business goals, work process change, and technology in determining plans. We also have a tendency to acquire technology in the same way as we did in the 1970s and 1980s, using Request For Proposals and long buying-cycles. By the time we reach a conclusion, the technology has changed twice, and so may have our business.

Building a guide for e-business ''e-commerce'' strategies is rather like producing a history course at the same time that the war is raging in the field. Difficult, particularly when the battlefield and tactics are changing frequently. We learn on a day-to-day basis, and need to take what we have learned to battle the next day.

We have never been faced with tools and strategies that can give us, in record time, direct access to so many consumers and customers or partners. Likewise, your competitors have never had such easy, direct access to your client base. Electronic information on all of us is being bought and sold to a broad range of companies targeting our purses and wallets. Similarly, the trends occurring in the B2B segment have already had a staggering impact on the marketplace.

All of this has led us to the current situation in the industry: pragmatism. With high failures rates, the higher cost of capital and a generally more conservative approach to e-business as a whole, appetites have become less voracious. Organizations want to drive risk out of their e-strategies and make the way forward to try to ensure that they build the ''right strategy'' not just ''shoot anything that moves.''

DON'T HAVE A CLUETRAIN?

In addition to the evolution of the business, some words have to be said about the huge changes in how business has been conducted as a result of the Internet. Nowhere is that better and more loudly said than in the bestselling book *The Cluetrain Manifesto* (Perseus Books, 2000), by several journalists and participants in the industry revolution: Rick Levine, Christopher Locke, Doc Searls, and David Weinberger.

Cluetrain is based on a set of 95 theses that set on edge the teeth of some traditional strategists. However, they clearly articulate how others are making their way through the digital jungle and that communities, conversations, and ultimately businesses and their decision making processes, have changed everything for ever. Excerpts such as the one below illustrate the power and irreverence of this book. Whether or not everyone likes the conclusions, they should definitely pay attention to the content.

> "The Web isn't primarily a medium for information, marketing, or sales. It's a world in which people meet, talk, build, fight, love, and play. In fact, the Web world is bigger than the business world and is swallowing the business world whole. The vague rumblings you're hearing are the sounds of digestion."

Much of the work in *Cluetrain* was focused on ensuring that the reader understands that people and communities make up markets when e-business technologies are deployed. Instant Messaging is as common a communication vehicle now for our children as the phone was for us, the key word here being "instant". Understanding that these elements cannot easily be controlled and manipulated is a fundamental pillar of the work. Even though published in 2000, many of the theses are as relevant today.

Here are three particularly relevant ones. You can investigate the whole set at www.cluetrain.com.

> "1. People in networked markets have figured out that they get far better information and support from one another than from vendors. So much for corporate rhetoric about adding value to commoditized products."

"30. Brand loyalty is the corporate version of going steady, but the breakup is inevitable – and coming fast. Because they are networked, smart markets are able to renegotiate relationships with blinding speed."

"63. De-cloaking, getting personal: we are those markets. We want to talk to you."

Cluetrain can teach us all something about not just alternative thinking, but how the Internet and its vast communication capacity has radically altered our world forever.

The E-Dimension

E-strategy and the Internet create new opportunities for managing and improving the way that business operates today. This chapter explores the key issues, including:

» strategy;
» the business case;
» business processes; and
» technology.

E-business is one of the fastest growing sectors of the world economy. One leading research firm (Forrester Research) estimates that business-to-consumer e-commerce will reach $184.5bn in 2004, up from $20.3bn in 1999, and that the B2B e-commerce market will grow to between $2.7trn and $7.3trn by 2004, up from $131bn in 2000. Displaying growth and momentum like this, it is little wonder that many companies and organizations are keen to join the e-business festivities. However, herein lies part of the problem. There is a tendency to look at e-business as a destination or an event. Whereas in reality it is a business strategy supported by technology and carefully selected business processes.

Developing new business strategies using electronic commerce systems requires three major ingredients. Strategy, business processes, and the supporting technology. Unfortunately, many organizations have developed and implemented solutions that do not effectively meet these criteria. This has resulted in disappointment, frustration, and "buyer's regret."

STRATEGY

A clear strategy for an e-business solution is the key to the door of success. Without a well-defined strategy the other parts may work, but not without significant revisions, out-of-control costs, and endangerment of the client base. Figure 4.1 illustrates this.

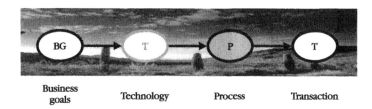

| Business goals | Technology | Process | Transaction |

Fig. 4.1   Key factors requiring alignment in e-business strategies.

Keeping these factors aligned ensures that the critical elements of the solution develop appropriately. However, careful does not have to mean slow, but it does mean that these important factors must integrate in a common plan. Developing and deploying an e-business strategy without talking to existing and prospective clients or understanding the demographics of the market can be, and often is, fatal. It is little different from building convenience stores miles from a busy road. No one would dream of it, but it is common to avoid planning with e-commerce systems. Assumptions are made, such as that everyone has a Web-browser and therefore everyone can reach us.

Reminiscent of the early days of automated workflow systems, e-business systems provide some similar challenges in ensuring that they are successful. Workflow required us to change business processes, apply technology, and roll them out in unison. So goes e-commerce, with some new wrinkles. To ensure that e-commerce systems are effectively developed, all parts of the puzzle need to be considered.

Table 4.1 below illustrates concerns that are on the shopping lists of many companies considering e-business solutions. Many things go wrong due to the poor development of a strategy. Like workflow in the past, most of these failures come down to three issues:

Table 4.1 E-business and strategy concerns.

People	Processes	Content	Technology	Transactions
Influencers	Sales process	The product	Infrastructure and development platforms	Purchase
Client (consumer)	Market feedback	The service	Security	Transactions
Client (business-to-business)	Advertising and promotion	Marketing and catalog information	Content management	Fulfillment
Advertisers	Customer support	Legal agreements and contracts	E-commerce	Shipping
Internal staff	Maintenance of site	Corporate information	Multi-language support	Taxation
		Multi-language content	Hosting and access	International distribution

» the business case for the system was not defined;
» it was doomed to failure because the business processes were not identified and agreed in advance; and/or
» the technology or the application did not prove suitable.

While there is still concern about the robustness of certain technologies to support demanding e-commerce applications, the first two items will cause most casualties in e-commerce. Avoiding these problems before they emerge is not difficult, but it does require some discipline.

Figure 4.2 below shows the benefits of taking a staged approach. This first step is to clearly understand the organization's needs. This step is the one often needed in e-commerce applications but most avoided. Understanding what customers want, and how they would like to have it delivered, is a great starting point for any strategy. This will provide insight, buy-in, and input to most of the application needs, simply by asking prospective users what they would like to see in the system. Once research is complete then the time is right to review the technology that is available to meet the e-commerce needs.

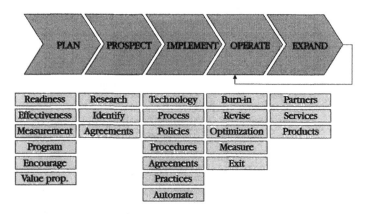

Fig. 4.2 Steps to consider in the development and deployment of e-commerce strategy.

THE BUSINESS CASE

Building the business case for the e-commerce strategy is a fundamental step for success. This can be as simple as a few bullet slides and a spreadsheet, but is a necessary step to building good solutions. E-business applications often provide very high Return on Investment, many producing returns in the range of 500–2000% or more. The successful ones create tremendous value for the organizations that use them.

Many models exist to develop a solid business case, but most require clear measurement of expected outcomes from the system implementation. Discussions and workshops are often used to ensure consensus and agreement in determining the outcome of e-commerce systems.

Hard benefits measure the positive financial impact to the organization, such as:

- » increased sales;
- » shorter sales cycles;
- » improved margins; and
- » reduced costs.

Soft benefits measure the less tangible benefits to the organization, such as:

- » improved competitiveness;
- » customer satisfaction;
- » better access to information;
- » better corporate image; and
- » increased staff satisfaction.

These are offset against incremental costs estimated as part of the development of the business case, such as the cost of:

- » hardware/software;
- » consulting (internal and external);
- » marketing and promotion;
- » hosting and Internet access; and
- » training and implementation.

Then, according to the accounting practices of the organization, the Return on Investment is calculated. Although there are always some variables later in the process, most of the opportunity has been quantified at this stage. This business case provides the foundation for the system development and deployment.

BUSINESS PROCESSES

The business processes to ensure success for an e-commerce application should be clearly defined. These can be as simple as defining site and product pricing updates, or as complex as defining B2B protocols and work processes with distribution and development partners. Part of the successful definition of the business case is to intensively review these procedures when determining the business case. What is the use of spending thousands of dollars on an e-commerce Website, and having no method to deliver the goods?

Some of the factors discussed above will help identify where to begin considering change in the process. Many of these factors may have little to do with the transaction itself, but can speed the decision making process, or accelerate sales cycles. B2B e-business represents a huge part of the marketplace. E-business provides the opportunity for companies to improve and cement business partnerships, and to develop new relationships by offering improved service and support.

Many business processes are linked to what are known as self-service or personalization applications. These are designed to provide information direct to the person who needs it without further intervention. Customer Support applications are very popular for these areas, along with a supporting Knowledge Base to provide the information to the customers when they need it.

Business processes cannot be ignored. If they are, e-commerce applications may actually increase costs and provide little or no benefit to anyone involved. The strategy will provide the drivers for change – new business processes must be developed to support it.

TECHNOLOGY

The majority of technology needed to develop e-business can be grouped into five categories. Application development tools are the foundation of any Web-based system. The majority of systems provide the technical platforms for system development and deployment. However, specialized systems have emerged into the marketplace over the last two years, dramatically reducing the time and effort needed to develop sophisticated e-commerce systems.

E-business development tools are impacting the speed in which very large-scale applications can be developed. Many tools now integrate inventory management, transaction security marketing, and catalog systems. Likewise, Content Management systems are providing organizations with the ability to deal quickly with customization, changes, and the controlled updating of Websites without the need for Web authoring tools. This is particularly important for international applications, needing different languages as well as content presentation in order to be effective.

The types of applications that are being developed include catalogs and product information sites, B2B applications, and self-service and customer service applications. These applications usually require careful control and presentation of information providing the most value to the target consumer. At the same time, they also require close control of the update, release, and approval processes for the information on the site.

The following list illustrates some of the categories of application types that are currently being developed using these tools, and the corresponding characteristics of those applications.

» Technical publishing, database publishing, knowledge management applications – high volume electronic document applications; built-in sophisticated information retrieval; and PDF generation.
» B2B communication, supply chain, distribution applications, and catalogs – customization of content and presentation can be controlled interactively; business rules can be developed and modified easily; high level of personalization.
» Commercial publishing, electronic magazines, and personalized content – customized content can be presented in many different forms and formats.

Security always raises its head as a concern on the Internet. More than ever, firms are concerned with security, viruses, and denial-of-service attacks (i.e., where a Website is targeted with so many requests that it shuts down trying to service them). Any time that financial information or internal corporate information is being accessed, companies worry about being breached. Firewalls, tunneling technologies, S-HTTP, digital signatures, and EDI all make continued strides to secure the Internet. We all want the openness and accessibility of the Web to market products, but we also want those private and secure transactions to be guaranteed. Despite these concerns, e-business is an unstoppable force in the marketplace.

The Global Dimension

E-strategy offers tremendous opportunities to go global. These include:

» the fundamentals;
» determining the business model;
» product suitability;
» pricing and legal factors;
» best practices;
» a matter of culture;
» getting the product right for the market;
» pricing and packaging; and
» why organizations need partners.

While writing this segment, I am on a plane headed to South Africa, my assignment to perform due diligence on a potential supplier for an up-and-coming fashion accessory boutique. The client's plan is to sell these products direct via the Web, as well as through specialized retail channels. Given these issues, the global reach of the Web is impacting how business connections are made, negotiated, and put into action. Suppliers and buyers are being connected in effective networks, creating new complications and challenges for the development and delivery of these systems. The speed at which these relationships can be established and their cost effectiveness creates a huge impact on how we can view business today.

The ability to reach out and touch at the global level is something that creates opportunities, and at the same time concerns others in the supply chain. The massive buying consortia of COVISINT are cementing global relationships in business networks that have more than $260bn changing hands annually. Speed can kill. However, it works both ways, you can be ruined by being too slow as well as by being too quick.

By now, most companies have implemented a presence on the Web. For many, an important aspect of this decision was the capability to go worldwide with their message and product. However, the global nature of the Web prohibits many firms from making "the big move" to international e-business. Important decisions have to be taken before putting regional price lists out there for the world to see. Many organizations have been scorched badly by their distributions and global operations as a result. In order to achieve accelerated sales cycles, potential clients have to see more information in order to make decisions quickly. Meanwhile, corporate concerns about comparative shopping and the public broadcast of previously "private" information, all gnaw at the current culture of the organization.

These issues and others come to the forefront when considering international e-business solutions. Determining the timing and methods to implement a program that will be successful can be a daunting task. The Web can be a shortcut, but there is a huge difference between an "informational site" and using the Web as an integrated part of a company's international business.

The road to success may be paved in part, but there are also some road repairs that can make the journey hazardous.

"In 2001, US e-commerce revenue is expected to reach $38.7 billion. Just 36% of dot-coms are pure-plays, while 63% are multi-channel businesses. Overall IT spend among dot-coms is expected to equal $15.3 billion in 2001. By 2006, when there will be an estimated 4,000 dot-com companies in the United States, IT spend will decrease to $9.2 billion."

Source: Datamonitor

With a vast international community of users and potential consumers, the Internet offers an opportunity that merchants and suppliers of information and services have never seen before. Today the greater numbers of users are still located in North America and Europe. However, new markets are also coming on strong as the impact of the Internet continues to grow. The number of users continues to expand across the globe.

For the development of the marketplace, obviously the growth and sophistication of patterns of users will determine how quickly expansion and adoption will happen. The high percentage of populations now gaining online access and increasing their buying activities will ultimately provide the foundation for the growth of the industry.

The most popular activities of users continue to be e-mail, finding information about a hobby, and general news. These continue to outrank online shopping as an activity, although this is growing in popularity. As it becomes easier to facilitate the delivery of goods and services, using the Internet and associated overnight shipment services, the convenience of shopping on the Internet is catching on fast.

Services that would not have been considered reasonable to purchase a few years ago are becoming popular. However, most of the sales to date have been in books, CDs, software, high-tech, and other goods which are easy to shop for and to deliver to the consumer. The range of offerings is likely to expand dramatically as groceries, financial services, and even online house-hunting expand their currently small penetration of the marketplace. Research shows for the first time some softening in the retail marketplace on the Web, particularly in the greater penetration that has occurred in the North American marketplace. However, the outlook for e-commerce still looks rosy over the long term.

THE FUNDAMENTALS

Several factors influence the development of an international strategy. These factors are often considered separately, but, for a successful implementation, should be considered in a common framework.

One reason why companies have taken time to make this move is the widespread impact to the organization, clients, and distribution systems. Considering international e-business, either as technology or as a better way of doing business, often leads to failure. Successful implementations consider both the business and technology factors as one.

Determining the business model

An international e-business strategy can dramatically change the way a company does business. Understanding the requirements for such a change needs careful consideration. Ensuring that this effect is dramatic in improvement and not traumatic to others is essential for success.

Usually one of the following three scenarios forms the basis of the business model.

1 A new international business on the Web.
2 Changing an existing international direct-sales business model.
3 Changing an existing international indirect-sales business model.

As Table 5.1 indicates, some major changes have to be considered in the development of this strategy. For companies that already have international distribution in place, channel conflict can be a major concern; for new distribution strategies the other concern of product support also will play a major part in the development of the strategy.

Product suitability

Ensuring that a product is suitable for the target marketplace is the next step in the process. This includes a number of factors that are specific for e-business, as well as others that are also important to ensure success. The following factors (source: Harvard Computing Group, 2001) are some of those that affect product suitability in the international marketplace.

» **Pricing** – is the product competitive in the local marketplace?
» **Competitiveness** – how should the product be priced and packaged for local market needs?

Table 5.1 Business model impact with international e-business (Source: Harvard Computing Group 2001).

Business model	Impact on direct sales to new international clients	Impact on current international channels	Impact on direct sales to current international clients
New international e-business model	No channel conflict, but complete system from demand through fulfillment has to be developed	Not applicable	Not applicable
Existing direct business model (non-Web based)	Could create conflict with current distribution systems in place, if not factored into the design	Not applicable	Could create conflict with current distribution systems in place, if not factored into the design
Existing indirect business model	Could create conflict with current distribution systems in place, if not factored into the design	Needs to be developed considering existing channels and support that is in place	Could create conflict with current distribution systems in place, if not factored into the design

» **Language** – is localization required to enter the market? What will be the cost and scope of translation needed for success?
» **Market size** – is the marketplace large enough to warrant the investment?
» **Internet infrastructure** – are there a suitable number of Internet users to make the transactions happen (including good connections via ISPs)?
» **Cultural infrastructure** – is e-business accepted as a means of doing business in the local marketplace? What is the current rate of e-business growth in this market?
» **Existing distribution systems** – are there current distribution systems in place that will help (or hinder) an e-business initiative?
» **Shipping/fulfillment** – how will the product be shipped and delivered to the client?
» **Support** – what local support is required?
» **Volatility** – is the market volatile (either financially or politically)?

A moderate amount of research should provide the information that will determine the most attractive markets to target. This will also provide some good input on the scale and cost of what is needed to customize your product or service to enter the market.

Pricing and legal factors

Developing pricing strategies for international distribution via the Web is no more complex (or simple) than any other environment. However, if this is the first foray into the international marketplace, then several issues need to be determined.

The first phase will comprise of the basic business issues of:

» single or custom pricing strategy for each market;
» margin goals;
» cost of sale;
» cost of support; and
» market share goals.

Once these have been determined, other pricing factors come into play, including:

» competition;
» what the current marketplace will stand;

» currency transactions;
» import duties;
» export duties; and
» shipping costs.

Many companies are concerned that once their US list price is shown on their site, then it will be very difficult to obtain a different (read higher) price from other markets. There is no question that once a US list price is shown, then a benchmark has been placed for international prospects and must be considered. However, there are other issues to consider that cause changes in price and support.

Some examples of these are shown in Table 5.2 below.

Table 5.2   Examples of variables and the impact on pricing strategies (Source: Harvard Computing Group, 2001).

Variables	Impact on pricing
Warranty	Increased price for international support
One single price based on US list	If the transaction is in dollars, no currency issues arise
Support	Local support has different price
Shipping and handling	Cost will increase based on client requirements (air or sea freight)
Customs and import/export duties	Usually paid by the consumer

Careful consideration of contract issues should also be made in order to avoid potential problems. A good approach is to keep things simple and understandable. This will reduce confusion and potential problems. Many countries have very different commercial trading practices, and it is important to become familiar with them before presenting them with an unsatisfactory method of purchase.

Legal professions and governments worldwide are trying their best to come to terms with the complex array of problems associated with trading on the Web. The Web changes many rules of trading that were based on the physical transfer of goods across borders for many years.

BEST PRACTICE

The development of an effective international e-business strategy is largely based on several factors. These include: thinking for the culture; improving business operations; protecting channels and the support they may give; and taking advantage of e-business opportunities.

A matter of culture

Of all things international, the cultural application of what should and should not be done remains critical to success. Because it is easy to offend through misunderstanding others' expectations and requirements, it is important to understand the very basis of the business deal. Far too many people fail to make the effort to understand international business concerns or are unwilling to adapt themselves to the realities of understanding cultures, customs, and languages in order to gain an advantage when doing business in different countries.

Successful organizations make the effort to understand how they are going to work together and the needs of their international business partners before they make their move. The businesses that do show interest in the people with whom they are dealing have found that it will lead to additional business. Just as an individual has to adapt to the relevant protocols of each nation to become an effective communicator and businessperson, so e-business needs the same adaptability.

Creating the right environment in the e-business system is also critical to meet the cultural characteristics of the marketplace. As many e-business systems require considerable automation of existing manual or physical processes (sales and service, for example), ensuring that these are acceptable to the target users and communities is essential. For example, the US consumer is much more likely to accept unsolicited mail, e-mail, and telephone canvassing for products. In Europe this practice is frowned upon, and the governments provide means for the individual to "opt out" of such systems.

In order to avoid some of these cultural issues, the following best practices can assist considerably in the acceptance of products and services.

1 Understand local business practices and how they can be encapsulated into e-business systems.
2 Ensure that the quality of language translation and terms and conditions meet local requirements and relevant laws.
3 Product packaging and naming should be sensitive to regional concerns and practices.

Getting the product right for the market

In simple terms, will the consumers buy the product? Is someone going to buy this product or service and be satisfied? These questions need to be answered in detail when it comes to the international marketplace. For example, on recent trips to the Middle East, a Web-based development service was being proposed for certain consumer items. However, when it came to the issue of fulfillment and the logistics of delivery the plan had to be halted. Why? Because the streets and the street numbering were so random, it became almost impossible to create a cost-effective delivery means. In the US or Europe this would never have been considered a problem, but to the logistics of the country in question this was a serious issue.

Factors for avoiding some of these problems include the following.

1 Delivery and fulfillment. Ensure that the product can be delivered effectively, to specific requirements of that market in a cost effective way.
2 Determine price and positioning points carefully. Many firms make the mistake of using the country of origin end-user price as the starting point for the development of the product line. Start out by understanding the retailer's or manufacturer's recommended selling price (MRSP), and reverse the margins and delivery means from there.
3 Try to avoid adding existing distribution layers (reducing profit and increasing overhead) to new e-business based offerings. While this is often difficult to manage, it will ultimately become a major factor in the long-term success of the venture.
4 Check out your suppliers, business references, and integrity. One disadvantage of Web-based commerce is that sometimes strategic relationships can be established very quickly. This can be a problem

when the qualification process lets less than desirable suppliers or buyers into your international supply chain. There is still no substitute for effective due diligence and visiting partners that are going to be critical to your international business strategy and ensuring they meet your own business standards.

5 Ensure your business partners and/or local staff understand the marketplace and product area that you are entering. This may be the most important factor in any overseas venture, as your business partners can provide you with the necessary intelligence to modify product or service strategy to meet the local needs effectively.

Pricing and packaging

In addition to earlier recommendations on pricing and packaging, the following should be considered as best practices in this very important area.

1 Test the pricing to meet the requirements of others in your supply chain as well as the final pricing in the marketplace.

2 Understand the impact of currency fluctuations and how they may positively or negatively affect the business model. Adjust the number of supplier locations if this is too risky for your business model (e.g., textiles, manufacturing).

3 Build the pricing strategy based on the operation's business goals. Adjust for market penetration and market share according to the competitive nature of your product line.

4 Ensure that your partners have a good business opportunity in your supply chain, otherwise they will only be short-term suppliers and partners to you.

Doing business in the international marketplace requires considerable effort, expense, and careful consideration. Many businesses fail in their first attempts to enter a new marketplace, and international commerce is no exception. Firms not willing to make the necessary investment to learn about the target market, and how they will successfully bring their product to that market, will ultimately suffer the disappointment of many who have traveled the same road.

PARTNERSHIPS AND JOINT VENTURES

Why your partnerships may make or break your e-business strategy

Anyone in business will tell you that good people, a great plan, and a hot market can make a company a huge success. Next on the list of important factors is the selection of excellent business partners. As organizations across the world determine the ingredients that can make or break their e-commerce strategy, partnerships are starting to be given new levels of recognition.

Over the years that pre-Internet-focused businesses have evolved, time was rarely the critical element for partnership development. Many organizations have focused on emphasizing the control of their partners' activities, paying less attention to the factor of time.

Why organizations need partners

Unlike earlier times in the computing industry, few firms can do it all. From marketing to hosting the site, there are many needs in the development of an e-commerce business operation. Moving from strategy to tactical implementation requires a lot of work, and most organizations do not have the bandwidth to bring all these pieces together in the required time-frame. This is particularly true in our current market conditions, where experienced staff are in short supply.

Real understanding of partnership principles is fundamental to formulating a B2B strategy. No amount of technology, Web portal infrastructure, or novel distribution strategy will provide real impact if the fundamentals of partnership selection and development are ignored. Our experiences in both Web and non-Web businesses is that some principles are the same. The paramount principle in any partnership is the concept of win-win. Despite all the negotiation, tactics, and bullying that occur in the business world, at the end of the day the partnership is much more likely to succeed if there is a win-win agreement. Trying to take the last penny out of the deal will cost more than what is saved in the long run. In today's e-business world, most firms understand that the run for market-share, mind-share, and customers is a sprint every day of the week. Joining forces and leveraging the power of many becomes a foundation for most operations' strategy.

The State of the Art

E-strategy technologies and the way they are being used is under constant change. The tools and ways they are being used is constantly evolving. So what are today's hot topics in e-strategy? This chapter explores current trends, including:

» e-marketing – what it is and how to use it;
» best practices;
» self-service;
» B2B;
» customer and partner support;
» distribution support and supply chain applications;
» affinity programs; and
» the one-to-many model.

Many factors affect the state of e-strategy today. We are all faced with considerable challenges on a daily basis, but finding a good way to resolve them continues to test our creativity and stamina.

As many businesses are now challenged with the issue of trying to change the way they operate, and sometimes very rapidly, the rules that have caused many businesses to become ineffective have rattled even the most seasoned corporate executives.

One problem with markets today is that the entry point can be considerably lower for intelligent newbies willing to disrupt the way that things were done before. Take eBay as an example, which started as an operation to focus on creating sales and exchange communities for collectors – they disrupted one market and formed another simultaneously. How did these collectors work together prior to eBay, what did we do with our clutter and extra items? Yard sales, flea markets, the local or regional classified magazine. eBay created communities that removed much of the distance issue, and formed communities much larger than any of the other means could have dreamt.

For most operations, though, e-strategy is only part of the operation: an important part but usually dealing with some existing business that needs e-strategy to help it along. With this in mind, this chapter deals with some of the most neglected, yet most powerful, concepts that e-strategy and e-business technology can impact. These are e-marketing, partnerships, corporate portals, and self-service technologies.

E-MARKETING

We have all learned the hard way that the Internet is, and should be, more than an online brochure. Continuous reminders from vendors, ASPs (Application Service Providers), and advertisements pound the message, but where should we start? Many organizations have assumed that e-marketing was the bailiwick of the chosen few, in particular those with high-end CRM and personalization tools. This is no longer the case. Effective marketing campaigns can be created and managed for much lower costs than with print or other traditional advertising channels alone. They can also be produced in record time-frames.

The foundation of the e-marketing strategy is created with a combination of offline marketing goals and, by using the Website as the hub, for all online activities. Often, the site can be used as the hub for the integrated online and offline activities of the overall marketing strategy.

The strategic design and effective management of e-marketing programs provide excellent ROI (Return On Investment) possibilities for organizations. Despite the claims of Internet marketing services operations, the most successful programs are those that are tied to the overall marketing strategy and integrated with traditional marketing channels.

Along with developing a program that is closely integrated with the overall marketing strategy, it is equally important to design a set of tactics, including processes, technologies, and tools, that can effectively support the program. For example, these tactics may include the use of partners in affiliate arrangements or the integration of the program with the organization's CRM system.

WHAT IS E-MARKETING?

E-marketing is the use of Internet-based electronic marketing systems to create awareness, demand and feedback, and responsiveness for the market acceptance of products and services. Increasingly these techniques are being viewed as an integrated strategy, where the ability to communicate, improve efficiency, and increase sales effectiveness is directly linked to the success of these programs.

Too often, many operations look at e-mail marketing, newsletters, print media, and the Web environment as individual and separate programs. Successful e-marketing programs start with well co-ordinated initiatives that link many aspects of the "electronic experience" for the Internet visitor. The foundation of these initiatives is the Website, where the hub of activities in e-marketing usually starts and finishes.

E-marketing does not have to mean "spamming" potential clients or abusing privileges to provide information to existing clients and to prospects. Targeted marketing and "permission-based" marketing are now the foundation of most loyalty-based e-marketing programs. These mean understanding both the needs and desires of prospective clients and modifying the messaging and information content to assist them in purchase- or information-based decision processes.

"E-mail marketing alone is experiencing explosive growth. Recent estimates from Jupiter Research indicate that email messages will balloon to 268 billion messages in 2005, more than 22 times the number sent last year (2000)."

Source: Jupiter Research

DEVELOPING AN E-MARKETING STRATEGY AND PROGRAM

Most e-marketing strategies are born as part of some major marketing program to create value as a result of the strategy. As with all effective marketing programs, marketing needs fuel for these programs, such as lead generation, brand building, cost savings, or market and revenue growth.

In the creation of any e-marketing program the following steps should be taken to ensure that the appropriate strategy will emerge based on the requirements of the operation.

1 Determine the role that e-marketing activities will play in the context of overall marketing activities.
2 Identify the e-marketing goals.
3 Once these goals are identified, a strategic outline will begin to emerge.

The creation of an effective e-marketing program should include the five major stages illustrated in Fig. 6.1 below.

A simple five-step program will assist most organizations in getting started with an e-marketing initiative. The first stage is to examine the context of the project – a careful review of how the e-marketing program is going to fit into the overall marketing program and how it should support the activities accordingly.

By identifying the specific goals of the program and the strategy that the organization is aiming to pursue, the next stages in the program can be more easily identified and implemented. Typical goals that might be on the shopping list of most organizations include:

» increased sales;
» shorter sales cycles;

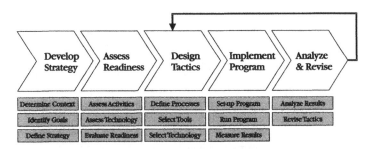

Fig. 6.1 An example of an integrated e-marketing program roadmap with actions at each stage (© 2001 the Harvard Computing Group, Inc.).

» client satisfaction surveys;
» improved customer retention;
» better communication with clients and prospects;
» increased Web-based traffic; and
» creation of new electronic communities and groups.

The e-marketing goals should directly support and assist in the implementation of the overall marketing goals for a product or service. There is nothing to be gained in trying to develop programs that are purely supplemental and developed independently of the general marketing strategy. It is, however, very important to ensure that these programs have measurable parameters by which to determine their success or failure.

Once these have been determined, a review of the current environment and the organization's readiness to use these systems has to be considered. Depending on the goals that have been set, the type of tool and program has to be designed. Understanding current capabilities and resources is an important part of this process.

Three factors will affect this assessment, and once it is complete then a "gap analysis" will provide a list of issues that need to be addressed to ensure the program will be successful. All e-marketing activities have three primary components: process, content, and tools.

While most operations have well-defined process and content creation means for print and other media, doing this from the Web perspective can be complex. For example, in the simple case of newsletter creation the ability to create areas of interest with hyperlinks allows readers to move into deeper content relevant to their needs. Also, by creating and tracking these links, sophisticated software will identify who clicked through to relevant areas of interest. Understanding how these tools work, what the traffic patterns are for the Web environments, and why the content is so important to the Web experience, is critically important to success.

Because organizations and individuals are bombarded with content in many shapes and forms, building a strategy that will produce results requires understanding plus the right tools and content.

During the development of the strategy plan, care is taken to define the processes and select the best tools for the job. As with most successful marketing activities, these fall under the umbrella of design tactics. This has several elements specific for e-marketing activities, including:

» defining the e-marketing process;
» selecting the right tools; and
» selecting the technology.

Defining the process will include the mapping of the various stages of creation of the program, from the content, editing, navigation, reviews, target audience, sourcing lists, determining targets, and how these will all play together. Mapping out the various stages of how others will interact with the organization's e-marketing program is critical to the success of the program.

The major elements in the design of the program are illustrated in Table 6.1.

These programs have to be set up in such a way that the tools and the processes make sense for the strategy behind the marketing program. The good news is that many of these tools can now be sourced using ASPs. These allow the set-up of sophisticated programs and management tools without the need to spend hundreds of thousands of dollars to do this in-house. This benefits the user both in terms of price and time to learn about these tools and systems.

Once the programs are in place, then detailed analysis of the results should occur immediately after the delivery of a specific campaign. As

Table 6.1

E-marketing activity	Tools
Website promotion	Search placement tools, registration, advertising, sponsorship, affinity programs
Measurement and feedback	Web traffic analysis tools, Web and e-mail survey instruments
Outbound marketing programs	Newsletters, e-mail, permission-based marketing activities
Campaign management	Integrated tools to measure and monitor success of previous activities and give recommendations to improve results

these results are digested, an action plan can be developed to capitalize on what worked for a specific area and what did not. E-marketing, like all marketing activities, should be under continuous refinement to find the best solutions. However, the programs typically provide returns that are much higher in effectiveness than print- or media-based advertising. Despite the tremendous cost-effectiveness of these tools, they are not a replacement for the traditional ones.

BEST PRACTICES

While e-marketing remains something of a mystery to many organizations, understanding how others have deployed these systems successfully is a great place for others to start. As with all effective marketing programs, the integration of customer data, content, and the delivery means determine the level of success in the programs out there. With today's ASP technologies it is possible to start small in these programs and expand based on capacity, needs, and proven results. The risks of creating a monster that will take over the operation and require massive maintenance are much lower than they were a few years ago. However, planning and tight execution are still requirements. Start simple, focus on the high-value returns and needs, and pick your partners carefully. These three rules will increase your chance of success considerably.

SELF-SERVICE

The Internet, and in particular B2B and B2C e-commerce, has produced some significant challenges for the development of rapid development of e-business systems. The recent advance of self-service applications has been used extensively in business exchanges and "infomediaries." Relationships for clients and partners that previously took months of research and visits can now be conducted in hours or days via the Web. However, making these relationships work and simulating and adapting business processes that were previously involved in on-site and face-to-face visits, have to be replaced and completed with new systems.

The answer has been the self-service solution. Organizations have built Web environments that target potential partners or clients, move them through the education and benefits of the products or services online, and ultimately facilitate the agreement or sale online.

What exactly do we mean by self-service? The Internet gives us such enormous value when we build the environment to support new ways of doing business. Of all of these, self-service is the most attractive business model. Beauty and business are not concepts that often go together. However, communications tools had a huge impact in previous technology revolutions. The advent of the telephone, the gramophone, and the television are all examples of self-service tools that improved communications and the range of our experiences. Because the Internet is multimedia, we have the chance to change the way that these interactions and experiences occur. By building systems that allow us to identify the transaction, the data, the people, the service, the results, it is easy to see how self-determination and selection is possible through the computer. We can provide the ATM, the research, the bank teller, the investment portfolio, the impact on our retirement plan – all in a single environment. The connection between research, decisions, transactions, and recording is all in one location. We can service ourselves, gaining advice and recommendations based on how to make the decision, then execute the decision.

To fully understand the importance of self-service, we first have to re-establish some principles that have not been in vogue recently. Due to the meltdown in many dot.com enterprises in late 2000, some bricks-and-mortar firms are feeling comfortable with their position of people-intensive systems, steering away from computer-based self-service models. Some consider that this model will continue, to the point that dot.com self-service has had its day. Forget this advice. Self-service is a strategy and technology that is not going away. It is going to become very large, and new and renewed companies will embrace it in a big way.

Being afraid of self-service systems may be the equivalent of a modern technophobe. Ignoring it will not just put the organization at a disadvantage – it could be considered mismanagement. The impact of these systems has been huge for the very large organizations that have implemented them, but we are still at the very early stage of exploiting their potential in the marketplace. There is a long way to go before we understand where this is going to end. But it is not going to end by ignoring technology and business processes that allow partners and clients to work more effectively together. By carefully selecting where to use self-service applications and techniques, many bland and ineffective experiences involving human interaction can be simplified and dramatically improved by the use of a self-service application.

The ATM effect

Imagine a world without ATMs. Standing in line for hours at the bank, wasting your valuable lunch hour. Remember when we could not withdraw cash during the evening or at weekends? It was a long time ago, but ATMs are self-service systems. Now add the Internet to the same principle: software downloads, music downloads, online banking, online stock trading, shopping for a computer, looking for a car, a home, etc. Increasingly, our society is going to the Web first for many of these requirements. Why? The Web provides us with the data we want, without having to interact with a sales person who is not adding value in their interaction with the client. We are serving ourselves.

The "ATM-ing" of the Internet is happening. Even organizations that have long held great control over the sales and support of their products are recognizing this, and doing something about it. A recent deal was made with General Motors and eBay. After years of trying to keep control of the entire supply chain and sales process, even the mighty General Motors recognized that self-service sales works with capital expenditures they thought would never occur.

Self-service dimensions

The full potential of self-service is leveraged when an organization considers the full gamut of business opportunities for its use. Whether we look at B2E (business-to-employees) systems, improving the way that employees can gather and reuse information, or sophisticated distribution channels, there are many ways of ensuring that the partner can interact with the organization.

Self-service has already been applied for distribution and support applications in many ways over the years. Some of these self-service applications have been less than satisfactory, as the quality of service (QOS) drops because of the introduction of self-serving applications. Telephony applications, long lauded by many as a great productivity improver, are a good example of technology used poorly. We have become familiar with (but not used to) long waits every time we call that reservation number for a flight, the long wait on the software company customer support line. Whether the call is free or not, waiting for assistance just makes the partner or client more unhappy. Most are unhappy with the result, so when the Internet and self-service applications let us serve ourselves improvements can abound.

Self-service applications allow organizations to achieve the following goals:

» improve the quality of service for applications that are repeatable and have defined procedures; and
» allow the volume of service to scale without adding large numbers of staff.

These two goals alone should place self-service high on the list of activities in the development of the partnership activities for the organization. Often self-service applications are relegated to those that cannot be developed with traditional systems, making the option of self-service the last stop in the line in determining strategies. Companies like Cisco and many dot.coms have reversed this trend, but realizing that there is no way for them to scale or provide the service to their partners and clients without self-service at the core of the strategy.

Self-service applications should be the ones that are sought out early in any partnership strategy. They will create value, codify knowledge, and improve customer service in a single stroke.

So self-service should be the first stopping point in the development of these systems. One major stumbling block for an organization in the development of these systems is reference points in the market. Whether Cisco can do it or not may not instill confidence in the furniture maker in Ohio, or the manufacturing company in northern England. As self-service systems require a complex blend of business, work processes, and technology understanding, they have to emerge from the initiating organization with confidence.

Part of this confidence can be built from a solid understanding of how the technology components work and interact. There is also a requirement to fully understand how work processes can be applied to the technology components in order to create the "electronic process" in a useful manner. That's the bad news; the good news is there are a lot of reference points out there today to look towards for guidance.

All or nothing?

Before moving too far along the self-service road, we also need to consider that self-service is a tool and not an end in itself. There is no reason why only a portion of a complete process or cycle should be made self-service, or complemented with other systems.

Customer service applications are good examples of this category. Where information is made available to the partner network and then an escalation procedure allows them to back out to get "real" help on the telephone or via on-site visits. For the early stage diagnostic aspect of self-service (troubleshooting and problem solving) the partner can enter this information direct via the support system.

Each part of the process can be defined according to what makes sense for self-service applications. Some simple self-service applications are in the category of a must-do. Downloads of corporate documents relevant for upgrading equipment in the field, material and safety data sheets, catalogs, etc., will usually not a take great deal of justification or analysis before deciding to make them self-service to your partners.

However, there are other cases where self-service will not be appropriate. As these occur, use other means and blend them into the process. In most partnerships, companies are looking for high quality responses in reasonable time-frames. By using self-service to automate many of these processes, improvements in time-frames and quality can be made simultaneously.

Self-service opportunities

Using a combination of technologies and new work processes, any organization can improve the way they operate internally, deal with partners, or support their clients using these systems and strategies. As outlined in Chapter 2, building your own self-service systems should start inside the organization. Not only will this produce the improvements that can create the platform for external systems development for partners, it has the added benefit of internal staff becoming familiar with the systems for their clients.

B2E – internal self-service

There are many different opportunities for internal self-service that can improve the way an operation works. Depending on the decision-making criteria for the operation, it may make sense for the operation to consider different applications to begin a project. As outlined earlier, self-service applications should be considered as another strategy and tool-set in the development process.

Organizations tend to have a wide range of technology and work process tools deployed in their employee development systems. To review where partnerships can be of most benefit, applications should be selected based on how much they can improve the way the partnership can be leveraged.

One of the top target applications for B2E that will ultimately create value at the partnership level is knowledge management. By organizing information inside the operation, based on improving the internal access to this data and then making it available via Web-based self-service technology, dramatic improvements can be made in productivity.

Whether staff are using this information to assist in product development, marketing, sales, or customer support applications, access to the right stuff at the right time will improve employee productivity and satisfaction. Sample applications for self-service in the internal organization include:

» accounting;
» facilities management;
» finance;
» human resources;
» internal IT support;
» knowledge management;
» payroll;
» pension and savings programs management; and
» telephone and partner directories.

Some of these will be easy to develop and deploy, others will require considerable security requirements and access controls to ensure they are deployed effectively (for example, the human resources applications).

Customer and partner support

Of all of the applications that have a huge impact on partnership relations, customer and partner support are usually the ones where tremendous return on investment lie. Because of the high cost overhead associated with customer support applications, it can be relatively easy for organizations to create ROI of 500% or more.

Taking applications such as a help desk, traditionally manned by telephone support, and moving many aspects of the service to the Web can change the entire customer support model for the better. Typical applications that meet these requirements would include ones that have a high number of procedural requirements, and of course some level of repeatability for the target applications.

Customer support has a potential abundance of opportunities for self-service applications. Increasingly these are also being made available in the ASP model, where organizations offer products that allow them to use their Web response platforms as a baseline for a self-service systems. This model, with many collaborative tools already included in the platforms, is becoming very popular for the development of partnership e-business systems. High-value applications that should be considered include:

» e-learning for distance learning;
» e-mail responses and bulletins;
» newsletter and e-service bulletins driven by sign-up mail list servers;
» knowledge centers;
» Web broadcast technology;
» online help built in to applications; and
» online policies and procedures.

Most organizations have focused on the low-hanging fruit of this application segment. However, planning in advance can save considerable dollars in the long run, and will also focus staff on dealing with the more severe problems as they arise. Most support staff do not enjoy having to answer the same question for the tenth time in a week. Capturing and reusing this information is key to the success of these systems, for both staff and the organizations interacting with them.

Sales and marketing

For the dot.com companies that started out with a Web-based sales solution, they have never had to deal with the issue of whether the sales process should be dealt with by people or whether they should be self-service. The reason for this is most dot.coms have had no sales process to protect, and many of them rely much more heavily on "electronic visibility" on the Web to gain partners and clients.

New-media magazines and individual industry periodicals have been the target of their advertising dollars, but much of the plan has been based on building partnerships via the Web. Affinity programs have become a mainstream way of gaining ground in the marketplace.

For the majority of organizations that are looking at self-service sales, a hybrid model will be in place. While Amazon does have customer account reps, their sales model is to keep these down to a minimum. With the exception of high capital items, spending a lot of time on the phone to support the sale of a $20 book is not a good use of their internal time. For that matter, it is not good for the consumer either.

Segmenting the sales activities so that elements of the process can be identified for their suitability to a self-service model is a useful exercise.

In addition, when considering these elements, it should be considered whether these elements will transfer to the potential partners' end-customer sales process. While this is an oft-neglected area, providing pre-designed sales processes and e-business models for new business partners creates tremendous value. Electronic stores and malls are a good example of how this can be implemented.

By reviewing existing sales cycles and processes, and identifying where the bottlenecks are in the processes, candidates will surface for self-service sales applications.

Most sales activities are tightly integrated with marketing activities in the electronic cycle. As e-business tools are used to assist with the development and identification of new prospects in the business cycle, they need to be tightly integrated into sales processes. This will ensure that they are not wasted.

Most self-service sales and marketing cycles focus on:

» shorter sales cycles;
» lower cost of sales;
» higher customer retention;
» cross-selling opportunities;
» faster qualification cycles; and
» self-service sales.

For partnership sales, the issue of who takes the order has always been a bone of contention. Depending on how the partnership has been organized, expectations for how sales will be handled, and by which party, will vary. In the case of business exchanges, where leads, buyers, and sellers intersect, the lead-giving organization will often take the front position. In other circumstances, such as a supply chain, leads may come from the partner to the supplier. In each situation, the optimized strategy will be dependent on these relationships.

By providing this information online it is possible to go well beyond the self-qualification stage, right though to purchasing and fulfillment of the order. Other opportunities in the self-service category would include:

» e-marketing;
» Web seminars;
» sales presentations;

» business exchanges;
» pricing;
» configuration management;
» inventory information;
» scheduling;
» shipment data;
» business intelligence applications; and
» market research.

The more sophisticated applications obviously require tight integration with some of the back-office systems data for inventory, product shipment, scheduling, and requirements for special orders. Companies such as Dell Corporation have brought this type of self-service selling to a new level in their direct client base, but have also optimized the back-office systems into their suppliers' systems to make the entire thing work.

Distribution support and supply chain applications

A major part of any partnership success, particularly distribution-oriented systems, requires access to much internal information for the partnership to work. The basis of many of these applications comprises information such as catalogs, price lists, configuration management systems, and all sorts of training and information transfer programs to support these efforts.

Fortunately, with the use of sophisticated content-management tools available in the market today, the same information can be reused time and time again. Many organizations have chosen to use self-service technology systems that allow them to reuse catalog information in many different forms. These are based on content-management systems that include the ability to syndicate the information content.

For these types of applications this apparently subtle difference is very important for the success of the system. By having this facility, the same content can be re-purposed to integrate into the partners' systems, even their own Websites, without modifying the original data. Even more impressive, using XML technology, the same content can be filtered for different languages, placement, and context. This is very important for any organization that is in the business of keeping this data up to date.

Other examples in this category include configuration-management tools used to assist partners to determine whether what they are planning to order will be available and what are the alternatives. Generally, the more complex the product, or the more sophisticated the range of requirements, the greater the need for self-service systems.

In recent months, the value of using e-learning tools and interactive collaboration systems to improve the way that an operation is running is also becoming a key differentiator in the development of partnership systems.

Organizations are beginning to understand that the development of partnerships is often measured in terms of when the partners exchange money, rather than when sign-up occurs. Distributed e-learning systems will help an organization transfer knowledge to its partners very effectively, gaining important self-service ground from competitors.

Affinity programs – power marketing of self-service

In addition to the standard agreements, percentages, and the coverage that a partner has as a result of your partnership strategy, we cannot build a program without considering affinity programs. Amazon almost invented this category on the Web, with their program starting in 1996, to allow others to put Amazon logos and products on their Website with the goal of creating click-throughs to their site, and then, of course, making purchases that the affiliate subsequently gets credit for. Amazon's affiliate program membership is currently approaching 250,000. A quarter of a million business partners! Most of these are managed via self-service software systems hosted on the Web. Imagine being the channels manager for that number of partners around the world.

Affinity programs are estimated to generate reference sales already of around 13% of all e-business sales in retail today. Industry watchers Forrester Research expect this to reach 21% by 2003.

They also rate higher in e-business effectiveness, well ahead of e-mail, PR, and other traditional media methods. A recent study by Harvard Computing Group draws comparisons between the very successful franchise models in the fast-food industry and today's electronic "franchising of the brand" through affinity programs. Time will tell if this is a reasonable comparison, but there is no question that these programs can assist a business dramatically.

What is an affinity program?

Affinity programs are partnerships between Websites. The Website owner who has developed the program is called the "sponsor" and the user of the program is the "host" or "target" site. Examples such as Amazon make it easy to understand how effective these programs are and how well they scale. Amazon builds its affinity program and then affinity partners sign up and receive payment in return for sales generated via site referrals (click-throughs) or banner advertising links.

Affinity programs are often compared to Web-advertising models that pay host sites a fixed fee per view (cost per thousand impressions or "CPM") or per click-through to the sponsor site. Some sites will use programs that are similar to paid affinity programs, for example not-for-profits, professional associations, and other certification endorsements. These programs can often follow similar self-service models; similar, that is, in all but the payment element of the program.

Affinity programs continue to evolve with the marketplace. Today, as the Web has evolved, so has the basic affinity program model. These include the following.

Syndicated e-commerce

In the past, shoppers and visitors were passed through to the sponsor's site via the "click-through" model. They would then place the order once at the destination. A syndicated model allows users to remain at the visiting site, by facilitating a "store" at their site. By keeping the users at the host's site, greater "stickiness" is achieved, as the visitor has no need to leave the site to complete the transaction.

An example of this model is Nexchange, which provides stores for their syndicated clients. By providing the shops to the hosting site, "look-and-feel" of the member's Website can be maintained, and their clients are automatically returned to the originating Website once the shopping transaction is complete. This will appear seamless to the end user.

Two-tier affinity programs

These programs allow affiliates to earn commissions by signing up new members of the network. By sharing commissions on this basis, new affiliates become agents for the sponsor firm. Companies such as DirectLeads pay affiliates 10% of the commissions earned as a result of their referral.

E-mail enabled programs

These programs have become more popular recently, by sponsoring e-mail programs. These affinity programs work as individuals attach advertising banners to their personal or corporate e-mails. This is ideal for individuals who do have Websites but want to take part in an affinity program.

B2B affinity programs

In July 1996 affinity programs started life in the business-to-consumer model, but there is a movement for new programs into the B2B marketplace. While still a relatively new area, programs from operations like www.Refer-it.com are entering the B2B market. Their B2B program has become very popular since its launch.

This category will continue to expand as others see the opportunity of offering office supplies, insurance, and other areas of interest to businesses.

Corporate intranets

B2B affiliate programs using corporate intranets as the target are rapidly becoming popular. This allows others to participate in revenue-sharing by placing links to the company's suppliers on the corporate intranet. By offering these links, companies can give employees preferred discounts and facilitate the use of specific companies' products that are known or preferred suppliers. Programs such as those from Linkshare allow this to be implemented and then track activities resulting from the program.

International programs

Affinity programs are growing in popularity in the international market-place. Companies like PlugInGo.com have established presence in

Europe, and Be Free has built a relationship with the media giant Bertelsmann.

Intermediaries and brokers providing the services to track the sales and pay out commissions to affiliates are further facilitating the international programs. Similar to the Web advertising world, organizations wanting to sponsor these programs do not have to set up the technology to deal with the hosting and tracking of activities. Companies such as LinkShare.com and Refer-it.com can provide these facilities.

Why affinity programs make sense

Affinity programs continue to grow in popularity as both sponsor and host site benefit from the relationship. The advantages to the sponsor include:

» increased sales with relatively low acquisition costs;
» increase in the sponsor's visibility in the market;
» leveraged distribution model; and
» expansion of the business network, creating new connections via self-service means.

Organizations that use host affinity programs also benefit considerably. Their benefits include:

» cash compensation for traffic and leads driven from the site;
» commissions from sales derived as a result of the program;
» improved brand awareness; and
» increase in the "stickiness" of the site.

Future trends in affinity programs

These programs continue to have explosive growth, and expansion across many markets will continue in the coming years.

The traditional development of these systems has been based on the one-to-many model. Allowing sponsors to create programs that are then delivered to large numbers of end-user customers has been the model of choice. While this works well in the B2C market, it can also be used effectively in a reverse situation, particularly for applications such as e-procurement and the like.

As organizations continue to become frustrated at the ineffectiveness of Web-based advertising, affiliate programs and how they are deployed will become more creative. Because e-marketing programs such as e-mail and newsletter are outrunning print and Web-based advertising, sponsors are looking for new ways to get their message out there. New destinations will be targets, such as internal sponsorships on e-procurement and electronic bill and presentation systems (EBPS).

Electronic bills are rapidly becoming the focus of many of these processes, including their print media brethren. Other locations and means to deliver these affiliate programs will test the creativity of marketers everywhere.

One-to-many and many-to-many models

In the B2B world, most goods today are still not sourced by surfing the Web. Most products are acquired through negotiated contracts with qualified suppliers or some spot market is identified to fulfill the need. Also, as many products purchased by businesses are components or unfinished goods, the B2C one-to-many model (see Fig. 6.2) does not have the same attraction as in the consumer market.

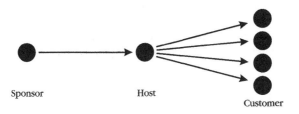

Sponsor   Host

Customer

Fig. 6.2   One-to-many model.

As a result, most business customers are likely to do their buying at a few predefined sites. These sites are likely to offer complementary content and have the potential of a many-to-many relationship (see Fig. 6.3). This will, in effect, create the conditions for expansion of an organization's business network.

As merchants continue to search for ways to reach the market effectively, new programs will emerge in this market. The connection

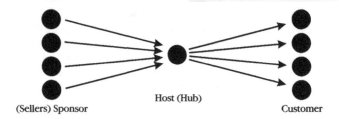

(Sellers) Sponsor Host (Hub) Customer

Fig. 6.3 Many-to-many model illustrating new characteristics of B2C programs.

between an interested and engaged consumer and their aversion to Web advertising continues to vex Web marketers. However, new affiliate marketing models, with syndicated content and product information, will likely supplant the traditional advertising programs.

These new e-commerce networks will combine media and seller sites with exclusive content to create differentiated and unique selling opportunities. Forrester Research has recently completed studies on this topic, often referred to as "elastic retailing." As the range of products and services on the Web continues to expand, the development of self-service applications that support these environments is sure to develop rapidly, particularly where differentiation between many product offerings is hard to discern, further illuminated by shopping agents such as MySimon.

Content remains king

Understanding the value of the content of Websites has moved from desirable to mandatory. Most organizations, particularly partner-oriented ones, understand this deeply. However, creating and delivering this compelling content is key to the success of affinity programs. Keeping a site "sticky" is critical to its success, and many organizations are turning to content syndicators to acquire the content to leverage and support traffic on their sites. Others are commissioning or developing original content to attract visitors and keep them coming back for more. Companies such as ScreamingMedia and YellowBrix are specializing in these areas.

Implementing self-service checklist

When it comes to implementing self-service, the following steps are recommended.

1 Develop a working group that includes management, operations staff, and IT groups from your organization.
2 Analyze and identify potential candidate applications based on support of strategic goals for the organization.
3 Review the technologies that will be needed to implement the system (and how others are using them).
4 Involve your partners in the decision-making process.
5 Define new work processes.
6 Specify requirements.
7 Build and test the system.
8 Educate internal staff and partners on the new system.
9 Roll out.
10 Refine.

Self-service may turn out to be one of the simplest metaphors for how to really use e-commerce technologies and work processes inside an organization. Easier than many technologies and systems, once explained, almost everyone in the organization "gets it." For this reason alone, it may be the Trojan horse that is required to bring the organization into the e-business world – a way of gaining management support and modifying culture without breaking all the glass in the store.

In Practice – E-Strategy Success Stories

What are the secrets of building a successful e-strategy system? This chapter explains how Federal Express, The Virgin Group, Cisco Systems, Altra Energy, COVISINT, and eBay have managed to use some of the most successful e-strategy systems in the market today. It includes case studies of their systems.

The leading organizations in the industry have made huge progress over the course of the past several years. Building and creating success in the e-strategy space has created some tremendous opportunities and results. In the early days of e-commerce and the Internet, the general thought process was that only those with fairly complex products or systems could make use of the technology and there was not much in it for the others. This created the original divide (now not so relevant), between the dot.com and bricks-and-mortar mentalities. One such example of a bricks-and-mortar company that transformed itself considerably thought the intelligent use of e-business strategies and systems is Federal Express, a leading supplier in the delivery of physical packages and related information.

FEDEX'S E-BIZ PHILOSOPHY

It does not take long to understand that Federal Express has an interesting view of its own strategic position. Just read this statement about the company's position in the marketplace: "FedEx Corporation provides integrated transportation, information, and logistics solutions through a powerful family of companies that operate independently yet compete collectively."

By the extensive use of technology to assist the way in which the company does its business, a continuous lead has been maintained in a competitive marketplace. FedEx tries to push the envelope (excuse the pun) in many ways with the use of e-strategy, along with the logistics of pushing and expanding their business operations.

FedEx realized early on that their business was more than delivering packages and goods to the right place in a very short period of time. By offering information services that provided logistic support for their clients' business, they have continued to expand and grow their services. The company has also developed a great brand in the market, with many considering the word "FedEx" synonymous with overnight guaranteed delivery systems. However the ability to integrate "FedEx" into all of the systems of their clients continues to allow them to differentiate themselves with their clients. More importantly, with an expanding product line, the depth of the relationship with their clients and the range of products have moved incrementally.

The latest statistics at FedEx.com illustrate the sheer size of the company's e-business reach:

» more than 2.5 million customers connect electronically with FedEx daily;
» FedEx currently have $12–13bn worth of business flowing through their electronic networks; and
» as FedEx deals with 1.2 million package tracking inquiries each day, huge savings are made compared to a mere 60,000 daily telephone calls into their call centers. This is producing savings of efficiency of more than 20 times the earlier manual processes. In July 2001, they estimated this to be worth more than $20mn per year.

Use of these self-service strategies causes the client to provide much of the labor to find the information, but most are willing to do this in order to gain instantaneous access to the right information.

Much of FedEx's expansion and growth has been tied to acquisition and effective integration of these services. They have:

» expanded their service offerings in target markets;
» created value-added information services that can be amortized across the entire client-base, providing competitive advantage to their clients and leverage of core competencies; and
» continued to expand their business integration systems, positioning the Fedex.com portal as a common point of access for clients.

While now more than 30 years old, the company's embracing of both technology and the Internet to leverage the way they operate has become somewhat of a model in the industry.

Another major facet in the recent growth of the company has been a focus on globalization. Here, with sites localized in many languages, the company can produce new content and services and bring them to market in short periods of time.

FedEx has taken the concept of self-service systems and really put it out to work in the marketplace. Most customer service functions are now available via the Website: tracking, shipping, billing, relevant rates. Most of the concerns and information that prospective and existing clients want are there in one location. By raising the information bar,

FedEx continues to keep its competitive edge and wants to try and stay ahead of the competition in a tough marketplace.

THE VIRGIN GROUP AND RICHARD BRANSON

We are reviewing Branson here, not because he has been the best proponent of the Internet, but because he epitomizes a "contrarian" view regarding strategy in general.

Branson's collection of companies shows that vision, drive, and not accepting the status quo can create huge value. He also has "larger than life" marketing skills in creating useful and relevant PR for his operations. However, despite this, he has been able to create value, loyalty, fun, and money in his strategy and work. How many companies that started out in the recording business (Virgin Records), would have even dreamt of diversifying to the extent that Branson had done, let alone almost making it appear like strategic policy?

Few businesses have operated with this model successfully, but if the market shows an opportunity for a differentiated product, and the current supply chain, service, or competitive situation is assailable, then Virgin appears to be able to move in.

While Virgin Trains may seem like a stretch, the other companies and services do have some synergy together. Whether that was part of the grand design or not, the reality is that Virgin has been very successful in many business areas that others may have considered impossible tasks.

CISCO SYSTEMS

Long held as an example of how to develop businesses effectively in the Internet era, Cisco could certainly teach most of us a lesson in how to leverage technology as part of e-strategy. It almost invented the concept, realizing early in their history that using internal technology effectively was going to be vital to their success.

As a global supplier, Cisco has manufacturing plants in many countries, and managing this network of plants, suppliers, and business partners is critical to the company. Its supply-chain system, supported by a powerful e-business system, has made a huge impact on its bottom line. As early as 1998, the company reported savings of $500mn by using these systems effectively.

Cisco has used configuration management and online ordering systems since 1997. These tools help its business partners select and configure, get pricing information, and conduct B2B e-business. Cisco has been the poster child for operations using the Internet for internal and business partner efficiency. The company claims to have saved $1.5bn in 2000 through increased operational efficiency and cost avoidance. With B2B sales of more than $19bn, Cisco represents one of the largest e-business companies in industry today.

Cisco is a special type of company, one that truly understands not just how to leverage the Internet as an e-strategy advantage, but one which appreciates that it is fundamentally core to its business and cultural operations. Because most of Cisco's growth has been based on increased market share, employee satisfaction, and a huge number of acquisitions (more than 40 at the time of writing), Cisco knows how to integrate value into the operation. Cisco has consistently proved its ability to change technology, work processes, and strategy in unison. Therefore, despite being large, it is able to respond to market changes much more effectively than its competitors.

The internal systems at organizations such as Cisco provide information that is relevant to clients and partners in a very short period of time. The collaborative systems that Cisco has built to assist partners and clients in solving problems for themselves online have created a very large economy of scale when it comes to bringing products to, and supporting them in, the marketplace. At the internal level, Cisco also uses self-service for issues such as expense reimbursement. Self-service, however, is only one aspect of success at organizations like Cisco. The culture of supporting clients and focusing heavily on the company's success is also key to Cisco's rise to stardom in the IT industry.

While much has been written on the topic of Cisco's leading self-service strategy, the company has been hugely successful because it understands the issue of process change for the merger program. In a world where many employees are unhappy with their workload or their treatment by employers, Cisco stands out. A recent survey put Cisco as the best company to work for in the United Kingdom. The company has such a strong culture that people really are important, that loyalty and productivity from its staff beats many others in the business

The corporate culture and the willingness to change has been central to the successful integration of many smaller firms since 1993. By placing dedicated teams to assist with the transition of new firms entering the group, few can boast of such an outstanding record as Cisco's, particularly with a relatively low level of attrition as a result.

While Cisco does not leave newly acquired firms to their own devices, it also does not miss out the fact that, of the core reasons why they made the acquisition in the first place, it is the people that make up the operation.

ALTRA ENERGY

While selling excess gas over the Internet might seem like a silly thing to do, Altra has proved it can be done. In fact, Altra has proved it six billion times in the first half of 2000, a transaction volume that would make many exchanges envious. Building an exchange that brings producers of excess energy to hungry buyers has proved very fruitful for the company. By providing a trading platform where buyers and sellers can meet to trade natural gas, gas liquids, power, and crude oil, Altra has been a very successful exchange in the marketplace.

A private company based in Houston, Texas, Altra Energy Technologies, Inc. offers an electronic marketplace, along with a suite of products to schedule, transport, and account their energy transactions. In addition to facilitating the purchasing process (using systems that separate the buyer and seller until the transaction is complete), Altra also offers portfolio monitoring and scheduling of trades for their clients. E. Russell "Rusty" Braziel founded Altra in 1996, as business units of the Williams Companies and Duke Energy Corporation were consolidated, creating what has become the world's leading energy software and e-commerce company. As with most successful private exchanges in the market, the industry knowledge and personnel have provided the underpinning for a successful operation.

With several years' experience and a strong position in the marketplace, the future for exchanges such as Altra looks bright. By bringing the parties together that were not trading effectively with each other, and selecting energy products that are particularly suited to this form of trading, their huge niche has been well established.

COVISINT

When looking at e-strategy initiatives, the picture would not be complete without looking at large consortia and exchanges. During 2000 and 2001 there were many casualties in the development and delivery of Web-based exchanges. However, there are still more coming to market. One that has gained the attention of the media has been the huge buy-side consortium from DaimlerChrysler, Ford, General Motors, and Nissan/Renault. Named "COVISINT" to indicate a strategy of *co*nnectivity, *vis*ibility, and *int*egration, the B2B hub could be the largest transaction engine this side of the New York stock exchange. Transaction revenue estimates have run as high as $240bn over time. With this level of volume, the partnership has attracted the Federal Trade Commission's attention, with concerns about monopoly and price-fixing in the marketplace. For now, they have been given a clean bill of health, but this size of exchange brings buying power to new levels in the marketplace. The large auto firms have in general been late to take advantage of the Internet in the B2C space, but they really understand the value at the B2B level. Whether or not this consortium is successful in the long run, each auto supplier has been busy creating its own B2B exchanges to leverage its supply chain. As it becomes easier to find suppliers and partners around the globe, the big vendors want to ensure that their "chain" remains viable.

The partnership desires of consortia such as COVISINT are steeped in a desire to improve the time-line from design to a finished car from 42 months down to 12 to 18. While this is a noble cause, the other main reason is to drive cost out of the process. Most of this squeeze is likely to occur in the suppliers in the exchange, according to industry analysts. There are estimates as high as a 10% cost reduction for the vehicle production process. With companies like General Motors and Ford purchasing more than $80bn in supplies each year, you can tell that these partnerships are important to the future.

Time will tell whether COVISINT turns out to be the mega-partnership of the century. Certainly in terms of volume, with 90,000 potential suppliers, the exchange would be the largest in the industry, providing, of course, that they sign up.

eBAY

Creating one of the ultimate partnerships and consumer destinations in the marketplace today is eBay, arguably the world's largest on-line trading community. eBay is the epitome of the *power of many*. By creating an environment that permits individuals and small businesses to trade direct with each other, eBay has created a powerhouse in the marketplace. We examine eBay not because it is the biggest community, but because it has been able to create traction in a marketplace that has previously been hugely fragmented. While others failed to create the super-mall of the Internet, eBay has succeeded. At least if numbers measure success, with over 29 million registered users, eBay is a winner.

The entire philosophy of eBay is based on partnership and trust. They expect certain levels of performance in the description of goods from sellers, and that fulfillment works at the other end with buyers receiving goods. As its environment includes collectors, hobbyists, small business operations, antiques, and just plain lookers, eBay has a lot to deal with to create a compelling experience at its Website. During 2000, the community grossed over $5bn in merchandise; the company has also been expanding its offerings, moving into the B2B marketplace, and acquiring companies where it has not been able to provide services demanded by users of the existing environment. Half.com was one of eBay's 2000 acquisitions, combining auction and fixed-price trading on its site.

While the numbers making up its community are impressive, more important is that it has been able to provide a trusted marketplace for a community that had few locations available at which to trade their products. Flea markets, car boot sales, regional magazines, and classifieds were the locations where others could reach out and touch buyers and sellers. In a very short period of time, eBay has established them as a destination that meets many needs.

As with most successful Internet-based businesses, the company wants to leverage its brand and get more of the financial transaction from its clients and partners. eBay enables trade on a local, national, and international basis. It features a variety of speciality sites, categories, and services that aim to provide users with the necessary tools for efficient online trading. Areas of speciality include:

» eBay International – in addition to the US-based site, eBay has specific sites for the UK, Canada, France, Japan, and Australia;
» regional sites in the US market – this allows for the geographic segmentation of eBay items, particularly those that might be difficult to ship;
» vehicles from eBay Motors – one of the largest sites on the Internet trading cars, motorcycles, and accessories, this has become a destination site for all things automotive;
» the Business Exchange is eBay's entrance to the B2B marketplace – expanding rapidly, the site allows businesses to sell industrial and office equipment to buyers rapidly and easily; and
» a Live Auctions feature allows eBay to offer real-time online bidding for items that are on auction floors, creating new ways of connecting buyers and sellers to the traditional auction world.

Aside from the obvious volume and range of the offerings available from the eBay Web environment, the company has created some significant differentiators compared with others who are trying to muscle in on the marketplace. By continuing to move into new segments that have volume opportunities, eBay is connecting buyers and sellers in a very powerful manner. While individual sites are making a good market in small segments, eBay operates like a huge classified engine, flea market, and speciality store all rolled into one. While eBay offers these services at prices that users consider reasonable, it is hard to see how eBay will have its dominant position in this area challenged any time soon. The regional market expansion is particularly interesting, as the model can scale easily and also be customized to meet the specific needs of other areas rapidly.

eBay is expanding by providing financial services, along with the ability to acquire products and services through its channel. This mixed-selling model is rapidly taking the Internet by storm. Recent surveys indicate that as much as 50% of online purchases could be in the form of blended sales, where cross-selling of services occurs when others are in the presence of related areas of interest. Perhaps this will be eBay's next horizon on the partnerships front?

Key Concepts and Thinkers

E-strategy has its own language. Get to grips with the lexicon of e-strategy through the glossary in this chapter, and with some key concepts of leading thinkers in the field. This chapter also covers:

- » technology awareness;
- » market behavior and characteristics;
- » business model changes and verification;
- » culture; and
- » ambition.

While there are many concepts relevant to this topic, the following can help any organization with the successful development and deployment of their strategy and supporting systems. These concepts fall into these categories:

» technology awareness;
» market behavior and characteristics;
» business model changes and verification;
» culture; and
» ambition.

TECHNOLOGY AWARENESS

Organizations today are beginning to recognize the value of having staff, from the execs to the janitor, understand what technology is and how to use it. We cannot leverage e-strategy, without *many* having knowledge. Without this knowledge it is impossible for the organization to make intelligent decisions about *any* strategy. Ask any manager today if they are willing to invest in technology and most will say yes. Ask them to keep their staff up to date with how it will impact them and their competitors, and barriers start to go up. Excuses start to come out in droves: waste of time, non-productive use of already scarce resources – the list continues. However, it is clear that unless organizations understand what can be done by using technology effectively, then it will be very difficult for them to suggest relevant methods of improvement. How can there be improvement in systems if the managers and staff do not know where to begin?

Building awareness

Before leading into the technology components, the development of a strategy to ensure that staff can become aware of these systems is the starting point in this process. Education and revelation of how the technology can be used, where it is being used, who is using it, all create a baseline of knowledge to be applied in the strategy development. All too often it is the IT part of the organization that makes this investment. They then continue to advise the other parts of the operation where it should be used.

Big mistake. While it is critical that the IT function understand what technology is available, and where it may be appropriate for the operation, they do not have an exclusive right to know. Of all the divisions that typically reside in an operation, this information gap is one of the widest. The IT staff do not understand what are the processes and procedures in the departments, and the departments do not comprehend what the technology is and what it can do for them. Unfortunately it does not end there – the most uneducated of all (except in high-tech or dot.com companies) are often the executives themselves.

So now you have it, three groups with different views of what the technology is and how they can use it. A foolproof recipe for mistakes and misunderstandings. Little wonder consultants have been having a heyday in this market trying to run interference in this confusing mess. The good news is it does not have to be so. A solution is at hand known as technology awareness. Training and education programs that provide to all of the staff potentially affected a clear view of what the technology is and how to use it, allow for the development and implementation of systems that will really change the way the operation is running.

Technology awareness will be a fundamental weapon to effect change in organizations wanting to take advantage of the Internet and build business networks rapidly.

Technology awareness is not complex, it is not expensive, but it is an investment. Many organizations still view training as a factor *after* the system has been developed, not before. But without awareness of what can be developed, and more importantly where it can be used to improve the business, outcomes are often first-time failures. By spending some time in the early stages, staff will understand where the technology can be applied, and as a result will gain the benefits accordingly.

Creating a seminar-based technology awareness program will speed the decision cycle, process change, and ultimately the adoption of the new system. Without it, learning becomes more iterative, therefore slower, and of course, more expensive. As many partnerships are based on speed and accuracy of results, this can be punitive in nature.

To develop and deliver a technology awareness program, the following elements should be included to ensure a successful outcome:

» build, select, and deliver technology awareness programs that will educate your staff on the key technologies in the relevant areas;
» include examples of technologies and how others have used them in relevant ways;
» illustrate work-process change;
» show how channels and partnership systems have added value to others in the use of their systems;
» do not use a vendor of systems to deliver the program; and
» allow staff members to contribute and interact during the sessions – this is particularly important to ensure that questions are encouraged and that they are answered effectively.

Consulting operations are increasingly using technology awareness as the first stage in the development of strategies and programs for their clients. As more change is required by the organization, it is more important that this is conducted early and effectively.

MARKET BEHAVIOR AND CHARACTERISTICS – MARY MODAHL, JACK TROUT, AND STEVE RIVKIN

In her ground-breaking book, *Now or Never*, Mary Modahl illustrates clearly the change in thinking that is required to ensure that we are not playing in markets that have rules that are clearly defined or "easy." Given the number of failures that have occurred in many organizations' first Internet attempts, the concepts and issues raised in her book would seem to be validated.

Modahl predicted considerable change in the behavior of consumers, the characteristics of which have already been codified by a methodology from her then consulting firm, Forrester Research: "technographics," which focuses on the demographic characteristics of consumers and their attitudes toward technology.

Understanding Internet consumers

Understanding why, when, and how different people shop online is the first step to winning the battle for Internet consumers. Unfortunately, likely online shoppers and unlikely ones look at first to be very similar in age, occupation, income, education, and other characteristics traditional marketers use to predict consumer behavior.

Based on considerable research, Modahl illustrates how online consumers' attitudes can have a big impact on the adoption rate of any technology, in particular regarding the Internet and shopping online. When the original research for this book was done, the division between pessimists and optimists was fairly evenly divided. However, the important concept here is to ensure that the audience for your product or service is going to provide enough traction for the success of the business model. Otherwise, you could spend millions without any reasonable prospect of success due to consumer or user attitudes.

With segmentation and details too rich to cover in this overview, Modahl articulates the differing stages of market development to consider when bringing an online product to market. The relationship between economic, attitudinal, demographics, and technical skills has a big impact in the success of any system.

DIFFERENTIATION

Differentiate or Die, by Jack Trout and Steve Rivkin, published by John Wiley, is a focused piece of work that assists the organization make changes that are most relevant to the current market conditions. With over a million branded products in the market today, Trout argues that many consumers have more choices than they know how to handle. All of this leads to the development of real differentiation in order for them to flourish and survive. He recommends a four-step process to achieve clear and defensible differentiation for any product line.

Step 1 – make sense in context

Arguments are never made in a vacuum; there are always competitors swimming around you, making arguments of their own. Your message must make sense in the context of the category; it must start with what the marketplace has heard and registered from your competitors.

You need a quick snapshot of the perceptions that exist in the market, and from that snapshot you can discern the perceptual strengths and weaknesses of yourself and your competitors as they exist in the minds of your target customers. You must also pay attention to what's happening in the market, to gauge whether the timing is right for your differentiating idea. For example, Nordstrom's idea of "better service" played perfectly into the context of a department store market that was reducing its people and service as a way of cutting costs.

Step 2 – find the differentiating idea

Your "differentness" does not have to be product-related. There are many ways to set your company apart – the trick is to find that difference and use it to set up a benefit for your customers.

Consider Hillsdale College, near Detroit – one of thousands of post-secondary institutions in the United States. Hillsdale has constructed a differentiation strategy based on the fact that it does not accept any Federal aid for grants and student loans. The college's pitch is "We're free from government influence" – a successful argument that has positioned Hillsdale as a Mecca for conservative thought.

Step 3 – have credentials

To build a logical argument for your difference, you must have the credentials to support your differentiating idea, to make it real and believable. If you have a product difference, you should be able to demonstrate it, and that demonstration, in turn, becomes your credentials.

Claims of difference without proof are simply empty claims. A "wide track" Pontiac must be wider than other cars. As the "world's favorite airline", British Airways should fly more people than any other airline. When it's "Hertz or Not Exactly," there should be some unique service that others don't offer.

Step 4 – communicate your difference

If you build a differentiated product, the world will not automatically beat a path to your door. Better products do not win alone – a strong perception must be established in the marketplace to succeed. Every aspect of a communications plan should reflect your difference – your advertising, brochures, Website, sales presentations, etc. It is not possible to over-communicate your difference.

A real differentiating idea can be a motivational bonanza. When Avis said "We are only Number Two; we try harder," their employees were motivated to do just that. The differentiation factor can be even more important when it comes to the e-strategy. Keeping these differentiations to support real value propositions will ultimately validate many other aspects of your strategies.

CULTURE – PEG NEUHAUSER, RAY BENDER, AND KIRK STROMBERG

The cultural aspects of change for successful e-strategy implementation are often neglected. It is not possible for dramatic changes in strategy to have any significant impact without the help of the staff and how they interact. Leading organizational consultants have put together a blueprint for how to create the right conditions to reduce this risk area in your e-strategy programs.

Creating a culture that supports risk-taking

In companies where it is acceptable to take years to develop a product, everyone involved in the product is greatly insulated from risk. That's because each decision along the way is approved, modified, and revamped. But in the e-business era, the pace doesn't allow that luxury. It is no longer possible to take the safer, slower route. To thrive, companies and the individuals in them must be willing and able to take risks.

In risk-encouraging cultures, people are rewarded for taking risks. It has to happen at every level within your company, not just among an elite group. To make risk-taking one of your dominant traits, you must:

» encourage it by providing monetary and recognition rewards;
» reward risk-takers whether they succeed or fail, but reward successes more highly;
» loosen the controls over decision-making so people can make more decisions on their own;
» let teams do their jobs without bureaucratic interference; and
» hire proven risk-takers and let them lead

Making decisions at warp speed

Decision-making goes hand-in-hand with risk-taking. To increase risk-taking you must make it easier for your employees to make decisions. They have to be freed to move rapidly. To encourage faster decision-making, begin to cut the number of meetings or approvals needed to reach a decision. Remember, people tend to fill any amount of time allotted for a task. To speed the process, cut the allotted time, while ensuring that the authority to make the decisions stick is in place.

As you make the changes necessary to speed decision-making, remember that it will not be easy. Allowing more freedom and releasing control from bureaucratic overseeing is one of the most difficult changes leaders working in traditional companies make. Upper management needs to ensure teams are staying within their strategic focus, but not interfere with the details of how the teams are carrying out their mission. Often, organizations that have the ability to change rapidly have a broader job definition and strategic goals, and allow the management to "achieve goals" without a game-plan dictated from above.

The deepest layer of culture

The underlying assumptions and core values are the hub of the wheel for everything else about the culture. Examples of underlying organizational assumptions include whether the group believes society should be organized around the community or the individual and whether it is acceptable to do several things at a time instead of finishing one task and only then moving on to the next. Generally, underlying assumptions are unspoken.

Core values, on the other hand, are conscious and discussed or written about in the organization. Examples include statements like "Customers come first," "Individual initiative is the source of success," and "Keep your promises. Your word is your honor." Keep that in mind as your company makes the transition into the e-strategy program, while core values should be aligned with the new requirements.

Behaviors and habits

The behaviors and habits of people working for your company make up the middle layer of culture. These are the company norms and include everything from formal policies to the informal tactics employees use to get things done. Formal policies may include everything from dictating behaviors like always answering the phone within three rings to requiring that workers never bypass their supervisor when seeking permission.

AMBITION – JAMES CHAMPY AND NITIN NOHRIA

Well, what does attitude have to do with e-strategy? A huge amount, as it does with any strategic situation and opportunity. Aim for defeat and you will likely get your wish. James Champy, head of Perot Systems and co-author of *Re-engineering the Corporation*, teams with Nitin Nohria (Harvard Business School) to produce a book on a topic that we often leave from the e-strategy mix – ambition.

Ambition and how to use it effectively is an amazingly important ingredient in the development of any organization's strategy. Some of the important pointers from Champy and Nohria include the following.

» **Seeing what others do not** - an ambitious person believes that hard work and transforming an idea into a workable solution is key. Others will follow if the path is laid well.
» **Following a steadfast path** - despite setbacks, it is crucial that the business continues down a path of perseverance, optimism, and unadulterated hope to make the moment of opportunity come to life.
» **Seizing the moment** - when the opportunity is out there, taking action is the most important factor for the winners.
» **Tempering ambition** - stay balanced with power/ambition and how they are used to achieve the goals of the operation. Often, as individuals reach higher levels of success, they become too enamored with their own achievements.
» **Never violating values** - maintaining the values and qualities that make up the business operation and its strategy is most important, especially when there are opportunities to cut corners just to move ahead.
» **Keeping control by giving it up** - the only way to keep control is by giving some of it away. Fear chills minds and kills companies.

» **Changing or perishing** – change is inevitable. Do not become complacent, or the competition will whittle away at your success.

All of these factors will have some impact on the development of your e-strategy programs and systems. None of them will provide a solution on their own, but together they will assist in reducing the risk in the development of the final implementation.

GLOSSARY

Bricks-and-mortar – a term used to describe traditional stores and methods of selling and distributing products. Barnes & Noble, who sell books through their stores as well as online, can be described as using both bricks-and-mortar and e-commerce strategies in their business.

Brochureware – the act of putting your corporate literature in basic static form directly onto a Website. Often bores visitors to death and causes rapid exits from the site.

Business-to-business (B2B) – the portion of the Internet market that effects transactions between business operations and their partners in marketing, sales, development, manufacturing, and support. The largest portion of the Internet marketplace, and the fastest growing.

Change management – the program to define, implement, and refine the changes required for the business to effect a change in strategy, process, and technology. Used extensively in existing bricks-and-mortar organizations to assist staff in the transition to new business practices.

Channels – can have two meanings in the Internet context. A "channel" is a Website designed to deliver content from the Internet to your computer, similar to subscribing to a favorite Website. Typically, it is not necessary to subscribe to the Web, but by connecting to the "channel" suggested content can be delivered to your desktop browser. Secondly, "channel" is used in the sense of a distribution channel, a method of providing your product or service to the target user of the system. This could be an online mall, portal, your own brand site, or distribution supply chain.

Clicks-and-mortar – organizations that have bricks-and-mortar (traditional non-Internet-based businesses) which have changed their strategies to provide both online and offline channels for their clients and business partners.

Click-through (or "click-thru") – the act of clicking (with a mouse) on a particular graphic or element on a Web page. Clicks are measured to determine the effectiveness of advertising, content, and traffic patterns of individual Websites.

Community – electronic forum where individuals and groups gather to find relevant and pertinent information. They are often segmented by interest or geography.

CPM – cost per thousand impressions. A measurement of how many times someone has viewed your banner ad via a Web browser.

Customer relationship management – technology systems and internal processes to support the continuous relationship with clients from early stage prospecting through to customer support. Typically providing support for sales, marketing, support, finance, and increasingly workflow processes, to allow clients to serve themselves with information and product.

Disintermediation – being excluded from a business network or supply chain due to new market conditions, pricing or distribution processes, and operations. Usually happens when the value being provided by the organization is not high enough to prevent getting squeezed out of the chain.

Early adopters – groups of users and individuals that will typically adopt technology and new work processes early in their introduction to the marketplace.

E-business – term now used broadly for the act of doing business using the Internet and other electronic means.

EDI – electronic data interchange. The controlled transfer of data between businesses and organizations via established security standards.

E-tailing – online sales of retail-style goods. Many consumer and specialist goods are now available via online e-tailers.

Extranets – private wide-area networks that run on public protocols with the goal of fostering collaboration and information-sharing between organizations. A feature of extranets is that companies can allow certain guests to have access to internal data on a controlled basis.

E-zine – online publications in the form of newsletters or magazines that allow for a new way for communication and interaction to occur on the Internet, e.g. www.salon.com

Impressions – the number of times that an element of a Web page has been viewed by an individual browser. Often used to count Internet ad placements.

Intranet – an Internet-based computing network that is private and secure. Typically used by corporations, governments, and other organizations, these are based upon Internet standards and provide the means for an organization to make resources more readily available to its employees online.

Legacy Systems – generally described as an existing computer system that is providing a function for some part of the business. Often, these systems are considered older in nature, but often provide some strategic function to the business. Examples include: inventory management systems, manufacturing resource planning systems (MRPs), enterprise resource planning systems (ERPs), sales automation systems, and help-desk systems.

One-to-one marketing – customization and personalization of both product and prospect requirements to meet an individual set of established needs. Once matched, a one-to-one marketing program delivers an exact marketing message, with the appropriate product to meet the prospect's needs.

Personalization – customization of Web information to specifically meet the needs and desires of the individual user.

Portal – major visiting center for Internet users. The very large portals started life as search engines. AltaVista, AOL, CompuServe, Excite, Infoseek, Lycos, Magellan, and Yahoo! are examples of major portals. B2B portals offer locations for individual business transactions to occur specific to affinity groups and business needs.

Pull technology – describes the type of technology used on the Internet, where users search for and request information to be downloaded to their computer.

Push technology – delivery of information to potential consumers via electronic means. Often involves the automated transmission of new data on particular topics on a regular basis, or some predetermined event.

Quality of service – defines the level of service for an individual, voice, data, or video connection when using a telecommunications supplier.

Stickiness – a general term to describe the characteristics of a Website to attract and keep users in the area. Also a measurement of how many users return to the site for more information or products.

Targeted marketing – development of marketing programs by identifying segments in specific markets and designing the product or service to specifically meet those needs.

Telnet – allows users to log on to different computers and run resident programs. Although this is not as lauded as the World Wide Web and requires commands to navigate, it is essential for Internet travel.

Tunneling – a secure mechanism to allow transmission of data across points of access on the Internet.

Resources

Much has been written on the subject of e-strategy. This chapter identifies the best resources including:

» Websites;
» portals;
» books; and
» journals and articles.

RECOMMENDED READING

» *Blown to Bits*, Philip Evans & Thomas S. Wurster; Harvard Business School Press.
» *Blur: The Speed of Change in the Connected Economy*, Christopher Meyer & Stan Davis; Capstone.
» *Culture.com*, Peg Neuhauser, Ray Bender, & Kirk Stromberg; John Wiley & Sons.
» *Customers.Com*, Patricia B. Seybold; Times Books.
» *Cyber Rules: Strategies for Excelling at E-Business*, Thomas M. Siebel; Doubleday.
» *Differentiate or Die*, Jack Trout & Steve Rivkin; John Wiley & Sons.
» *Enterprise One to One*, Peppers & Rogers; DoubleDay.
» *Fast Alliances*, Larraine Segal; Wiley.
» *Flash of Brilliance*, William Miller; Perseus Books.
» *Inside the Tornado*, Geoffery Moore; HarperBusiness.
» *Net.gain*, John Hagel & Arthur G. Armstrong; Harvard Business School Press.
» *NetSuccess*, Christina Ford Haylock & Len Muscarella; Adams Media Corporation.
» *Net Worth*, John Hagel & Marc Singer; Harvard Business School Press.
» *Now or Never*, Mary Modahl; HarperBusiness.
» *Six Sigma*, Mikel Harry & Richard Schroeder; Random House.
» *The Customer Revolution*, Patricia B. Seybold; Crown Publishing.
» *The Fifth Discipline*, Peter M. Senge; Doubleday.
» *The Strategy-Focused Organization*, Robert Kaplan & David P. Norton; Harvard Business School Press.

In addition to these excellent book resources, some resources for specific topics are listed below. These will provide up-to-date information on particular e-business areas that are changing and evolving rapidly.

E-STRATEGY AND E-MARKETING

The following are excellent Web-based resources for e-marketing activities.

eMA – e-Marketing Association

The eMA is a professional organization for companies and individuals involved in the practice of e-marketing and the integration of online and offline marketing activities. This site provides resources such as white papers, newsletters, Web tools, and articles, as well as information about professional certifications. The site can be accessed at: http://www.emarketingassociation.com

Wilson Internet – Web marketing & e-commerce

This site, created by Ralph F. Wilson, is one of the best free sources for e-marketing resources on the Web. The site includes a large collection of free articles, a newsletter, and recommended books, all highlighting e-marketing best practices. This is a great resource for organizations currently using the Internet as a key component of overall marketing strategy. The site can be accessed at: http://www.wilsonweb.com/

Brint.com – e-business

Brint.com has long been recognized as an excellent resource for business professionals. The site includes a section devoted to e-business, in which many relevant topics are covered, including a directory of Web-marketing resources. This page can be accessed at: http://www. ebiztechnet.com/cgi-bin/links/links.pl?passurl=/Computers/Internet/ Marketing/Resources/

KNOWLEDGE MANAGEMENT
KMWorld

KMWorld is the leading information provider serving the knowledge management systems market. The site provides information about the components and processes – and related success stories – that together offer solutions for improving your business performance. The site can be accessed at: http://www.kmworld.com/

Knowledge Management Magazine

This magazine's site is an excellent information source for the latest developments in knowledge management. The site can be accessed at: http://www.kmmag.co.uk/

Brint.com – knowledge management portal

See above. The site also includes a portal devoted to knowledge management, which includes forums, magazines, articles, events, resources, analyses, and news. This page can be accessed at: http://www.brint.com/km/

RE-ENGINEERING

Re-engineering Resource Center

This site is an excellent information source for both the re-engineering novice and the seasoned professional. The site can be accessed at: http://www.reengineering.com.

Brint.com – business process re-engineering & innovation

See above. The site also includes links to information about business process re-engineering, which includes papers, books, articles, and tools for process re-engineering. This page can be accessed at: http://www.brint.com/BPR.htm

PORTALS

CIO.com

This site bills itself as "The Leading Resource for Information Executives." Topics covered by CIO.com are organized into "knowledge centers." Although there is no specific knowledge center for portals, a search for "portal" will turn up hundreds of articles on the subject. The site can be accessed at: www.cio.com

Intranet Journal

The *Intranet Journal* is an excellent source for information on portals as well as other technology utilized by intranets. The site offers access to articles and case studies as well as an intranet events calendar. The site can be accessed at: www.intranetjournal.com

Ten Steps to Making

E-Strategy Work

Building a successful e-strategy solution requires a plan of action. This final chapter provides some key insights into creating and implementing an e-strategy solution in today's business environment, covering the following steps:

- » change practices;
- » workflow – how work is managed;
- » work patterns and practices;
- » impact awareness;
- » inclusion;
- » disclosure of the facts;
- » collaboration and involvement;
- » change readiness;
- » culture and how it affects your strategy; and
- » building in best-practices.

Preparing a company for dramatic change requires many of the skills and strategies outlined in this book. While we can apply some of these principles based on what others have achieved in the process, one of the most important elements to achieve is how to mitigate risk.

Being ready for change and making it happen are two distinctly different things. We have to get ready to send the raft down the river at some time. If we control the boat and can steer it, this is as good as it gets. If the river is the market, the tide can be smooth, wild, or downright treacherous, depending on the circumstances. Every organization has to make the choices, weigh the risks and rewards, and decide how much to change and how quickly, all the time keeping a careful eye on the moving marketplace. There is a reason e-commerce strategists and managers are well compensated, as this is a challenging ride.

In addition to devising the right blueprint, the willingness of an operation to make the necessary commitment to embrace the current industry climate is an ongoing challenge.

RISK AND THE CORPORATE CULTURE

All businesses start with a vision. This overriding vision should direct where the company or organization wants to arrive and over what period. The starting point, then, is to create defined goals from that vision that can be measured and adjusted on a continuous basis.

While much of any strategy does rely on planning, resources, technology support, and execution, attitude can still be pivotal. Cultivating a "can do" culture without terrorizing staff and managers is a balancing act. Try comparing a new e-strategy initiative to a merger or acquisition. Successful acquisitions have very aggressive cultural and system integration programs, many of which measure successful integration over three to four months. This is because once more than three months have passed, the ability to impact the new organization becomes more difficult. Making the sort of change that is required in the Internet today often requires some hard swallowing.

Many look for a "magic bullet" when it comes to implementing a radically new business plan. Our first realization has to be that there is no magic bullet. Regardless of the status of one's business, every successful enterprise is built around people and the way that they work together. However, we can learn much from the tools and techniques that others have used to "get there" quickly. In doing so, we also have to recognize the difference between deliverables that occurs because someone transported us there and those that we brought directly upon ourselves.

Searching for this blend is a key factor in the current economic situation. Businesses are beginning to recognize that their assets are tied up in people and how they interact, not just in the bottom line. In a world that requires us to be smart, flexible, predictive, and able to execute, people are the deciding factor. And, of course, how they are encouraged to behave.

The change in the post-industrialized world is well articulated in *The Fifth Disciple*, by Peter Senge, where we see that the learning organization becomes the most valuable over time. So how can we progress from the plan to the action? A critical examination of work and how you want it to be processed in the enterprise is an excellent place to start. The way we deal with work, in new and imaginative ways, ultimately supports our plan.

1. CHANGE PRACTICES

Defining what needs to change is one thing, burning it into the organization is another. Ensuring that new practices and attitudes are effectively infused requires some blood, sweat, and tears. Making change happen requires some key elements in the implementation process including:

» developing a plan to integrate all the elements of the new strategy;
» tight integration with new work processes, technology, and business goals;
» an education and change-transfer program at all levels in the organization that require it; and
» adequate staffing and resources to make new business practices and processes take hold.

Many traditional bricks-and-mortar organizations are giving up on the idea of radical change occurring within their organizations. This is primarily due to the difficulties of implementing it in the necessary time-frame. Many new e-strategy programs require a seek-and-destroy approach to existing practices, distribution channels, and ways of operating. Sometimes this type of change can be too much too fast for existing business units.

The development of new systems and processes requires a clear understanding of what happens in the market if the organization does nothing, or executes poorly. The scare factor can be an important motivator in Internet times. After all, inadvertently arriving second in the market may be debilitating to a currently successful bricks-and-mortar business trying to make the transition.

2. WORKFLOW – HOW WORK IS MANAGED

Workflow is a word that means many things to many people. Some use it as a definition of the technical changes required to build the new systems and support the business practices. Others consider workflow to be the internal management of systems and work packages.

For the purposes of this section, consider workflow as a method of defining new ways of doing business. Every business, no matter how complex, has a set of written (or unwritten) rules that define how business is done. By building and defining new work patterns, it is possible to encapsulate how business is done prior to the new system and thereafter. A work plan can help implement this sort of change in an organization; it becomes a very important element to consider in the development of new ways of doing business.

As your plan evolves, implementation becomes the key factor. Can the plan be implemented, and how do I effect the required change in the organization? The level of change management required to cover the range of options here is well beyond the scope of this book. So many organizations have differing needs, and the amount of internal and external change varies dramatically. However, the use of workflow as a method to manage change can be a useful and practical tool.

And again we'll recommend an integrated approach. There is little or no point trying to change one element of the organization without the supporting components from other parts of the Go To Market (GTM) strategy.

Building and supporting customers in this manner requires us to think in a multi-dimensional way, not required before the Internet.

The idea of someone starting as a prospect, then making a sale, and then having to support the customer in a very short period of time is amazing. This type of behavior is exactly what gets enterprises very excited about the change ahead.

For these reasons, workflow is a good way of getting to grips with how to start the change process within your organization. Each group within the organization will have a before-and-after work process, and these changes need to be carefully documented and explained. It is not good enough to lay out goals and then not provide a vehicle for the staff responsible to make them happen.

This modeling of the workflow does not have to be too complex, but it has to be consumable. If we can't explain to others what we are trying to do, then what is the chance that they will be successful in making this take place? Another useful aspect of this process is determining the crossover of functions between groups and activities in the e-strategy process.

The work process definition is on the path to gaining staff and business partner buy-in of the process. Without this, get ready for some major modification after your first release of the system. Market testing of these new workflows will make a huge difference in minimizing risks.

3. WORK PATTERNS AND PRACTICES

As new workflows are developed to support the GTM strategy, a detailed analysis of what they are and how they will be implemented needs to be prepared.

One of the hardest areas to deal with is existing work practices. A good e-strategy will do its best to collapse and eliminate unnecessary work practices. Just because something is working well today does not mean that it is not a candidate for change. Every aspect of the business that can be improved should be reviewed as a potential candidate for change.

As discussed during earlier chapters, preservation of certain factors can be very important to the success of the enterprise. These include:

» business ethics;
» integrity;

» quality; and
» service.

The core standards of the business are often sacrosanct, and obviously maintaining them is critical for any success, whether with old or new business models.

Other practices, however, have to be placed on the table for consideration. Table 10.1 shows some examples of factors that may be changed as part of new work practices of a B2B strategy, and why they make sense.

Table 10.1 Examples of old and new work practices and their impact.

Old Practice	New practice	Change	Why it makes sense
Cold-calling via phone for prospect generation	Self-service sales qualification process directly on the Website	Electronic and self-qualification process supported via the Web	Lower cost of sales, shorter sales cycles, broader market appearance, scaleable approach
Telephone help desk as first line support	Knowledge-base serviced via the Web	Client uses self-help area on the Web and has access to all the relevant information on corporate knowledge-base	Better service to the client, faster, more scaleable, lower cost
Invoices sent manually to client as billing cycle demands	Electronic billing via the Website	Client has to log in to check on the status of invoice and billing information	Scaleable, lower cost, improved service, history information, data in electronic form, easily customized

The remaining steps in this chapter look at several ways of ensuring that all appropriate members of the business are fully on-board.

4. IMPACT AWARENESS

In earlier chapters, the need for technology awareness was reviewed. Understanding what is out there and how it is being used is a major factor in getting staff and the team on the same page. In addition to the technology, we have to look at how it will impact the organization.

The impact awareness should include some candid discussion of what may happen as a result of the new business processes. If it is determined that the change is too large or too fast to assimilate, some serious review has to be considered. (Perhaps a separate group has to be considered to implement this level of program.) Hierarchical management structures have the biggest problems with these changes. E-strategy plans cannot be managed from a lofty "command-and-control center." The plan has to be adopted, believed, and supported by those who are going to implement it.

Impact awareness will allow staff to understand what is the likely outcome in the development of the plan and program. Management is unlikely to have all the answers, outlining the game plan, why it makes sense, what would happen if we sit and do nothing, and other potential outcomes. Impact awareness should draw analogies from other industries where they are not evident in your market space. The qualities of speed, flexibility, and collaborative execution have to be brought to the forefront.

5. INCLUSION

The issue of inclusion often stops managers and executives in their tracks. Who to involve and when comes down to a combination of control, business judgment, and personal style. While presenting plans and programs before the need is established can be dangerous, conversations regarding these issues are probably already going on in the organization, but may not be reported at staff meetings.

While the level of inclusion can be determined by ability to contribute, also consider the objectives of the program. The goals are likely to be driven more by ensuring that the best ideas are surfaced, percolated, and agreed. The origin of those ideas is less important than leveraging them.

6. DISCLOSURE OF THE FACTS

Once decisions have been made on involvement, give staff the straight facts. The times when staff could be protected from bad news and a changing environment are long gone. As your plan will likely have involved many different groups inside and outside the organization, disclosing news is an important element of ensuring that it will be adopted.

The absence of facts can result in key staff departures and lower productivity, both of which impact on the ability of the enterprise to be effective.

7. COLLABORATION AND INVOLVEMENT

Involvement is the only way to create an integrated system and effect change. This does not mean that every decision will be dealt with and delivered by consensus – after all, most enterprises are looking for very high-impact changes when considering new work practices and programs.

The collaborative forum(s) can vary according to the style and requirements for the operation. One excellent method widely used in industry today is the workshop. This can be particularly effective, providing some good homework has been done up front, so that participants can spend their time reviewing and documenting new ways of doing business. Some forums and their purpose include those in Table 10.2 below.

An important aspect of the collaborative process is keeping the process alive all the way through the development and deployment of the systems. After all, new work practices have to be adopted and tested by those who are agreeing to use them in the first place.

8. CHANGE READINESS

Being ready for change is one of the most important people-and-process aspects of doing business. As many organizations have reward systems that do not genuinely encourage risky behavior, and have a tendency to punish failure at most levels, some significant relearning is often required. Change readiness is about informing staff that there are new rules in place in the organization. They need to be encouraged to make changes and suggestions; they should not be concerned about being "shot down" because of new ideas and refinements to the system.

Table 10.2 Examples of collaborative forums and tools.

Forum	Purpose
Brainstorming sessions	Open sessions on a particular topic (sometimes no topic), where ideas are presented and discussed according to their relevance (or irrelevance).
Workshop	Excellent method of taking information and ideas previously identified and creating a framework where they can be reviewed, refined, and prioritized according to the business needs.
Bulletin boards	Electronic versions of brainstorming or review sessions. Can be very formal or very informal according to topic review.
Mailing lists	Topics are circulated among groups, and responses posted for all to continue to follow a particular thread.

Change has to be viewed as the normal way of doing business, and that the operation can consider itself in continuous transition, one to be encouraged. Developing programs in the organization to make this the normal mode of operation is crucial to success.

9. CULTURE AND HOW IT AFFECTS YOUR STRATEGY

The impact of culture on an organization is truly profound. As most managers in the e-business space today have come from the non-Internet era, the reference points for decision-making have been classical in the making. While many executives like to think of themselves as entrepreneurs, few have really made it to that mindset.

One reason in many is the standard frame of reference taught over many years in business and at universities. We have come to understand programmatic and structured approaches to every aspect of the development of a business, along with a considerably static market. Therefore, we have many businesses with a predetermined culture of operational standards. Many of these are very useful, but others have habitually resisted the required degree and pace of change. This is particularly evident in organizations that have predefined reward systems that drive how the company runs. The large consulting firms are a good example of how this corporate culture can work against an organization in today's economy. Most of them are trying to find ways to redefine their businesses to move directly into this space and attract the supporting consultants to make it happen. Meanwhile, more Internet-based consultancies thrive in the market, with niche services to meet the needs quickly.

There are two schools of thought regarding how company culture should adapt to meet the challenges of the new economy. The first is: forget most of what you learned in the past and take a different approach. This is best articulated in a "bottom up" manner in *The Cluetrain Manifesto*. *Cluetrain* talks of new ways of doing business and interacting with customers. Concepts such as listening, delivering, supporting, refining, are given more play than the individual product message. It is required reading for managers who are still not aware of the new cultures evolving in this space.

The other school of thought will end up being a blend of current company practices adapted to meet the requirements of the Internet economy. The reason for the second approach is reluctance to make the culture leap required for the first challenge.

Table 10.3 below illustrates some of the problems that can occur as a result of static mindsets within organizations.

Failure to understand and address these issues will ultimately influence the organization's achievements. Many e-commerce productivity gains are based on effective behavior change in the enterprise, therefore it is critical to ensure that we link culture and process. Understanding these issues will dramatically improve the potential for success.

10. BUILDING IN BEST PRACTICES

If imitation is the greatest form of flattery, then certainly learning from others is a great way of speeding the development process of an e-strategy. Determining how best to develop and implement a strategy can be greatly enhanced through the use of best practices, as they are applied in your own and relative industries.

Table 10.3 Culture and work practice issues that affect deployment and success of e-business systems.

Example of culture	Result
Tremendous reward to individual efforts	More resistance to team-building and team rewarding initiatives
Entrapped in current work practices	Resistance to change
Hierarchical management	Difficult to adjust to collaborative team model
Driven by common corporate and employee goals/rewards	Rapidly adopt technology to support business and workgroup functions
Technology-driven	Needs help to assist with workgroup productivity and process issues
Technophobic	Needs significant persuasion to use technology at all

One problem with the Internet is ensuring that you do not end up just emulating last year's successes. However, if a program has become effective in an individual industry, then applying it to your situation can be an excellent way of improving your time to market and significantly reducing the risk of building a system.

There are several methods used to capture best practices, both inside and outside of the organization. Here are a few starting points in the development of your own system.

» Estimate the amount of resources and effort required in the organization for the solution to work.
» Review competitors in the segment that have built, or plan to build, similar systems. Look at any relevant methods that will assist in the development of programs.
» Build strategies and practices based around core business and organizational goals.
» Do not try to "boil the ocean" by including too much functionality or change in the first release. Research the impact of change in the organization and be ready to deal with it.
» Include resources for change management into the program.

» Ensure that new business practices are *burned in* after the new system is up and running.
» Stay away from technology-only solutions that do not support the business and work process needs of the system.

A major part of building in best practices is having a clear understanding of the cost and effort of change needed to occur outside of the organization. While new practices are easier to implement inside, most e-strategy systems require business partners and clients to change too.

Building in best practices requires a whole rethink of how we have done things in the past. We have to learn how to prototype, develop, test, and revise in real time. We have to ensure that flexibility, learning, and adoption of new ways of doing business, become core competencies of our business. In the same way that business rules and values support the operation, the ability to learn and change rapidly may turn out to be the most valuable skill of all.

Frequently Asked Questions (FAQs)

Q1: What is e-strategy?

A: See Chapter 1 for the answer and a look at how it is relevant to an organization and how it can be used to improve the way a business operates.

Q2: What are the world's most valuable e-strategy programs?

A: Chapter 6 shows the state of the art e-strategies and how they are helping organizations market, sell, and support their products most effectively.

Q3: Who is responsible for e-strategy development within an organization?

A: Who should be involved in e-strategy programs and how they can be built is outlined in Chapter 10, which suggests ways of making e-strategy work. See also the role of partnerships in Chapter 6.

Q4: I want to create and develop an e-strategy system. How do I go about it?

A: See Chapter 10, and also Chapters 4 and 5 for the e-dimension and global dimension of e-strategy.

Q5: What does the term "e-strategy" mean and why is it important?

A: Chapter 2 includes definitions of e-strategy, why it is key to any organization, and how to apply it in your organization.

Q6: How can e-strategy programs create value for organizations?

A: See Chapter 6, which looks at methods of successfully implementing e-strategy and e-marketing programs.

Q7: What are the best practices to improve the way that e-strategy operates?

A: Some key concepts of leading e-strategy thinkers are outlined in Chapter 8.

Q8: What are good real-world examples of successful e-strategy operations?

A: Chapter 7 looks at how Federal Express, cBay, COVISINT, and Altra Energy have successfully implemented operations using e-strategy.

Q9: How do I find out more about the subject?

A: Details of additional resources relating to e-strategy are in Chapter 9.

Q10: What are the origins of e-strategy?

A: Chapter 3 looks at the evolution of e-strategy.

About the Author

Michael Cunningham is the president and founder of the Harvard Computing Group, Inc., a professional services organization started in 1994 to develop consulting programs and tools that would change the timeliness and profitability of enterprise systems using Internet-based technologies. Often described as a "Business Technologist," Cunningham is that rare breed that can communicate how and when to leverage technology for business goals.

He is author of *B2B – How to Build a Profitable E-Commerce Strategy* (Perseus Books, November, 2000), *Smart Things to Know About E-Commerce* (Capstone, January, 2000), *Partners.com – How to Profit From the New DNA of Business* (Perseus Books, July, 2001), and *Smart Things to Know about E-Business* (John Wiley & Sons, October, 2001). Since 1994, Cunningham has been involved in the development of Internet-based strategies with HCG's client base, improving their operational efficiency, technology systems, work processes, business partnerships, and distribution systems. Cunningham's experience in partnership development has been ground-breaking. He is also a contributing writer for *E-Business Advisor*, with a column published bi-monthly.

His deep understanding of how to mix business goals, work process, and the effective use of e-commerce tools provide a unique perspective in the marketplace, one which HCG's clients have been able to leverage. His extensive operational and management skills have helped his clients through challenging transitions, providing new programs and business opportunities for their own clients. With over 20 years of experience in the development and delivery of complex software systems and their deployment, Cunningham is a sought after speaker and regularly contributes to magazines and publications in the information technology and e-commerce communities.

You can contact him at:

Email: mcunningham@harvardcomputing.com

Telephone: (+1) 978 692 6766 x204 (work)

Fax: (+1) 978 692 1864

Mail: Michael J. Cunningham

Harvard Computing Group, Inc.

238 Littleton Road,

Westford, MA 01451

USA

Index

Printed and bound by CPI Group (UK) Ltd, Croydon, CR0 4YY

13/04/2025

14656560-0004